After an affair, most couples  abound: Is this salvageable? Wh Will we ever be the same? In *After an Affair*, Michael Gembola offers concrete and soul-healing strategies so that both parties can benefit and grow through a better understanding of themselves and the gospel.

—**John Freeman**, Founder, Harvest USA; Author, *Hide or Seek: When Men Get Real with God About Sex*

Infidelity involves many factors leading up to betrayal. Deceit in behavior and in the heart are the two most obvious. Hidden sins require ruthless and consistent truth-telling as well as the risk of practicing new thinking and habits that will move people forward. Michael, in *After an Affair*, has helped us tremendously by outlining a thirty-one-day guide that invites us to do the deeper work necessary to target these hidden sins.

—**Penny Freeman**, Counselor, ServingLeaders Ministries; Counselor and Trainer, Parakaleo

When we're in a crisis, we need the hope of the gospel more than ever. But standard devotional guides don't seem to speak to the elevated emotions and despair we feel. This can make God feel far away when we need to feel him most near. That is why I am so grateful for Michael Gembola's devotional *After an Affair*. God's Word is sturdy enough for the most desperate times. This devotional is written so that the person swirling in guilt, shame, and life- and family-altering decisions can know that God will meet them right where they are—as painful and disorienting as that place may be.

—**Brad Hambrick**, Pastor of Counseling, The Summit Church, Durham, North Carolina; Author, *Self-Centered Spouse* and *Romantic Conflict*

After an Affair is a tremendous help to anyone who has experienced infidelity in marriage. Michael's pastoral wisdom and counseling experience shine as he directs the reader to spiritual food that is often missed but is critical to surviving the wilderness of adultery. I will certainly be recommending and using this resource in my own ministry.

—**Winston Smith**, Rector, St. Anne's Church, Abington, Pennsylvania; Author, *Marriage Matters: Extraordinary Change Through Ordinary Moments*

These devotionals are inviting and compelling. It is as if Michael is a good friend who knows you and knows exactly what you need. He will bring you into the meaningful words of God that give you direction, and he will set your pace so that you persevere with hope. By the end, you may find yourself wishing that a month lasted longer, so that you had more of Michael's helpful counsel to read—fortunately, the thirty-one devotionals here are well worth reading again and again.

—**Ed Welch**, Counselor and Faculty Member, Christian Counseling and Educational Foundation; Author, *When People Are Big and God Is Small*

AFTER AN AFFAIR

31-DAY DEVOTIONALS FOR LIFE

A Series

DEEPAK REJU
Series Editor

Addictive Habits: Changing for Good, by David R. Dunham
After an Affair: Pursuing Restoration, by Michael Scott Gembola
Contentment: Seeing God's Goodness, by Megan Hill
Doubt: Trusting God's Promises, by Elyse Fitzpatrick
Grief: Walking with Jesus, by Bob Kellemen
Pornography: Fighting for Purity, by Deepak Reju

AFTER AN AFFAIR

PURSUING
RESTORATION

MICHAEL SCOTT GEMBOLA

P&R PUBLISHING

P.O. BOX 817 • PHILLIPSBURG • NEW JERSEY 08865-0817

Italics within Scripture quotations indicate emphasis added.

Printed in the United States of America

Library of Congress Cataloging-in-Publication Data

Names: Gembola, Michael Scott, author.
Title: After an affair : pursuing restoration / Michael Scott Gembola.
Description: Phillipsburg NJ : P&R Publishing Company, [2018] | Series:
 31-day devotionals for life | Includes bibliographical references.
Identifiers: LCCN 2018033677| ISBN 9781629953908 (paperback) | ISBN
 9781629953915 (epub) | ISBN 9781629953922 (mobi)
Subjects: LCSH: Adultery. | Spouses--Religious life. | Marriage--Religious
 aspects--Christianity. | Devotional exercises.
Classification: LCC BV4627.A3 G46 2018 | DDC 248.8/44--dc23
LC record available at https://lccn.loc.gov/2018033677

Dedicated to my family

Contents

Building a Testimony

Qualities and Habits for the Long Haul

Tips for Reading This Devotional

EARLY IN OUR MARRIAGE, my wife and I lived on the top floor of a town house, in a small one-bedroom apartment. Whenever it rained, leaks in the roof would drip through the ceiling and onto our floors. I remember placing buckets in different parts of the apartment and watching the water slowly drip, one drop at a time. I put large buckets out and thought, *It'll take a while to fill them.* The water built up over time, and often I was surprised at how quickly those buckets filled up, overflowing if I didn't pay close enough attention.

This devotional is just like rain filling up a bucket. It's slow, and it builds over time. Just a few verses every day. Drip. Drip. Drip. Just a few drops of Scripture daily to satiate your parched soul.

We start with Scripture. God's Word is powerful. In fact, it's the most powerful force in the entire universe.[1] It turns the hearts of kings, brings comfort to the lowly, and gives spiritual sight to the blind. It transforms lives and turns them upside down. We know that the Bible is God's very own words, so we read and study it to know God himself.

Our study of Scripture is practical. Theology should change how we live. It's crucial to connect the Word with your struggles. Often, as you read this devotional, you'll see the word *you* because Michael speaks directly to you, the reader. The readings contain a mixture of reflection questions and practical suggestions. You'll get much more from this experience if you answer the questions and do the practical exercises. Don't skip them. Do them for the sake of your own soul.

Our study of Scripture is worshipful. I've never met a husband or wife who woke up one day and suddenly decided, "Today I'm going to commit adultery." If you have had an affair, it means that you started wandering from God long beforehand. You lost your orientation toward the One who should rule your life. Fundamentally, adultery is a worship problem. You, as an adulterer, are worshipping the wrong things. Here's where the Word helps: it points you to Christ, who rescues you from your plight and reorients your life. The goal of your time in the Word should be to reconcile yourself with God through Christ (see 2 Cor. 5:14–6:2). It is on that basis—a right relationship with God—that you can deal with the messy, painful, and hard consequences of your adultery.

If you find this devotional helpful (and I trust that you will!), reread it in different seasons of your life. Work through it this coming month, and then come back to it a year from now, to remind yourself how to do battle with adulterous desires.

This devotional is *not* meant to be a comprehensive guide to dealing with the fallout from adultery. Good volumes are already written for that purpose. Buy them and make good use of them. You'll see several resources listed at the end of the book.

That's enough for now. Let's begin.

Deepak Reju

Introduction

I'M SO SORRY you've had to pick up this book. I would not wish it on anyone. In the days just after the disclosure of an affair, everything is complicated and embarrassing. You feel misunderstood. It's hard not to feel nervous about the next hard conversation. Is separation (or worse) coming? Finances get wrecked. Family and friends are distant. You have God alone to turn to. And maybe He's not too happy with you either. Feels that way, at least.

This book is for people who have been unfaithful to their spouses and who want help. It's for people who want their souls and marriages to be saved.[1] My goal is to help you better understand the God who saves and the kind of life that paves the way for reconciliation with your family, even if you feel little hope that reconciliation will happen. I write primarily out of my experience with counseling Christian men, though the core principles will apply to women too.[2] My prayer is that you will find these words truly devotional and that you will experience God's closeness and a renewed sense of His calling on your life.

The fact that you've started a devotional suggests that you believe two important things. First, you know that restoration is a process. This conviction is starting you on a thirty-one-day journey that I pray God will keep you on for years to come. Second, you believe there is something in Christian worship and devotion that is key to restoring your marriage. And you're right. Coming clean and coming home to God helps us to come clean and come home to our families, too.

This homecoming to Jesus unfailingly brings abundant life (see John 10:10). But He is much more than a means to an end. At the core of following Jesus is this conviction: there really is a

God, a good Father in heaven, who is deeply worth knowing—even during worst-case life scenarios. Today you may not know whether your dreams of being a family again will come true. You don't know the outcome. But you believe that God is in the picture, and He is active in writing a story—a testimony of His powerful work. Starting to tell this story honestly may *initially* make things worse. But coming to Jesus gets you where you want to go long-term. He alone brings your soul to safety.

God has promised that "all things work together for good" (Rom. 8:28). But I'm sure it doesn't feel that way right now. Consider it this way: God *causes* all things, which means intervening in all things—even in an affair—to work for good. He rips good out of the hands of evil. He takes upside-down things and makes them right-side up. *Even this.* One writer calls affairs "a disorder that leads to a new order."[3] Being honest like never before, and becoming oriented toward the love of God and others, leads to changed character and changed relationships. We're able to enjoy relationships like never before.

None of this is silver lining. There is no upside to infidelity. It brings God's wrath and everyone else's wrath. It's ugly and destructive. Since you already knew that, you are likely asking, *How could I have ever gotten here?* You're asking a good question—one that I hope you'll hold on to for a long time. The best way to avoid falling again is to understand what got you there and to make changes. This process requires new insights and efforts over the long haul to keep you on the right path. This will be the hardest thing you have ever done. But I promise you it is worth it.

Although God can instantaneously change us, His Spirit typically works through our gradual efforts in community and guided by His Word. You can think of the process as a struggle to find rest. It's like fighting insomnia in that it requires learning, changing habits, and then waiting. You can't do any one thing to force yourself to fall asleep immediately and get the rest you need. Similarly, after adultery, coming to a place of spiritual rest means finding new insights, acting on them, and waiting. It's a process that requires more patience than you've ever had to exercise before.

I wish I could offer you something faster than incremental steps. But God's people have often faced wilderness—long walks over long periods of time in hard conditions. Being different *over time* will be the only reliable indicator that you have really changed. If your marriage and life as a Christian are ever to thrive again, you have to be different—deeply and observably different—for a long time.

There is an important principle to remember as you begin this journey: *the normal progress of Christian growth is a process of gaining new insights and taking steps of action*. Gaining new insight is extremely difficult. It can cost us dearly. "The beginning of wisdom is this: Get wisdom. Though it cost all you have, get understanding" (Prov. 4:7 NIV). I will ask you to see things from perspectives you haven't yet considered—and to trust me that right now you don't see all that you need to see. Gaining new insight and a new understanding of God, others, and yourself must be a top priority.

I will first invite you to see God as the gracious, loving healer, in all the ways that He shines through the face of Jesus Christ (see Col. 1:15–18). I will also ask you to look with fresh eyes to see your spouse and to see the hurt caused by the affair. This is a miserable, painful, bad-tasting medicine, and I don't believe there is a way to add sugar or to make it taste anything other than awful. It's like chemotherapy. You will get nauseated and unbearably weary, but it's your best shot at surviving.

I invite you not just to gain insight and understanding but also to act. There will be some questions for reflection throughout, as well as tasks. Actions both change you and show that you have changed. Keep in mind 2 Peter 1:5–9 as a model of the action and insight required of you: "Make every effort [i.e., take action] to add to your faith goodness; and to goodness, knowledge; and to knowledge, self-control; and to self-control, perseverance; and to perseverance, godliness; and to godliness, mutual affection; and to mutual affection, love. For if you possess these qualities in increasing measure, they will keep you from being ineffective and unproductive in your knowledge [i.e., insight] of our Lord Jesus Christ. But whoever does not have them is nearsighted and blind, forgetting that they have been cleansed from their past sins" (NIV)

In the time leading up to, during, and sometimes long after infidelity, we experience nearsightedness and some degree of blindness regarding our Christian identity. We lose sight of and forget our family identity as the ones "cleansed from their past sins." And losing sight of this is still a danger for you, as you seek to move forward from infidelity. So remember, throughout all the hard work, that God cleanses people from their sins through Jesus. We must keep this before our eyes: He alone makes us clean, and we cannot save ourselves. And yet, the more deeply we know Jesus, the more productive and effective our hard work is. Out of the confidence that we belong to Him and have His love, we make every effort.

Forming a new pattern of life requires continual conscious effort, but it becomes more natural. After much hard work and reliance on the grace of God, you wake up one day realizing that you have been walking in a very different direction. What once felt impossible is becoming reflexive. You more naturally love what God loves. You more readily walk in step with the Spirit. These will be the moments when you sense that the Good Shepherd is leading you out of the valley of the shadow of death to green grass and waters of rest, and that you are excited to walk with Him. Let's take the first step.

STARTING WELL

When infidelity first comes to light, you may feel a mix of energy and discouragement. You want to try to make things better, but since the weight of it all can be so heavy, it's vital for us to start with words of hope. So we look to Christ as our healer, our only judge, and the one who ultimately will vindicate us. It's a long process, so you must find partners in the fight for your soul and your marriage. There are many obstacles, both outside and inside you. You may face conflicts with others and their expectations of your progress. You may grow weary and resentful of the process. Pace yourself for the road ahead, but don't give up dreaming that it leads somewhere truly good.

DAY 1

Faithful in Hope

What misery is mine! I am like one who gathers summer fruit at the gleaning of the vineyard; there is no cluster of grapes to eat. . . . The faithful have been swept from the land; not one upright person remains. . . . But as for me, I watch in hope for the LORD, I wait for God my Savior; my God will hear me. Do not gloat over me, my enemy! Though I have fallen, I will rise. Though I sit in darkness, the LORD will be my light. (Mic. 7:1, 2, 7–8 NIV)

MY DAD LIKES to go blueberry picking. He calls it his Saturday-morning therapy. I've gone with him before, and I see why he likes it. It isn't really fun late in the season, though, when all the bushes are picked over. It's a frustrating experience. You don't see much that is good.

When you look out on your life, perhaps what you see is this but much worse: empty bushes everywhere (see Mic. 7:1)—a picture of the devastation and bleakness that sin leaves in its wake.

The fact that you picked up this devotional means that you're the one saying, "As for me, I watch in hope for the Lord." Though you have fallen, you hope that in God's time you will rise.

We have a powerful enemy. He loves to see us fall. He would love for sin to be the end of us all. He'd love to gloat over us, especially when we sit in a dark place. If you feel trapped in a dark place as you're sitting here reading, remember this: while you sit in your dark holding cell outside the courtroom, inside the Lord Himself pleads your case.

Our enemy is our adversary in court. He wants us on the stand so that he can accuse us of everything and throw the book at us. "Has God not said _____ ?" He knows the Bible well, and he uses it to tempt us to failures in the first place, then toward despair after our failures. A job well done for him is a fallen saint discouraged. Is he getting to you? Do you feel hopeless?

You have the best Lawyer there is. And He begs the Judge for mercy on your behalf.

Reflect: What is your darkness? What dark thoughts and circumstances do you face today? Do you find yourself wanting to defend yourself from the accusations you face?

Act: Pray. Invite God to plead your case for you, and invite Him to give you the hope of light for as long as your darkness persists.

DAY 2

Faithfully Hopeless

To you, O Lord, belongs righteousness, but to us open shame. . . .
To the Lord our God belong mercy and forgiveness, for we have rebelled
against him. . . . We do not present our pleas before you because of our
righteousness, but because of your great mercy. O Lord, hear; O Lord,
forgive. O Lord, pay attention and act. (Dan. 9:7, 9, 18–19)

SOMETIMES WHAT HURTS the most is the feeling that there
is no way out of the mess you are in. Sometimes we have only
ourselves to thank for being in it, and we feel very little hope. In
the Bible we see pictures of God's people in these kinds of situ-
ations, and surprisingly, we see them asking for things that seem
almost too bold to ask. They have almost no hope—they even
have every indication from God that they stand under judgment.
And yet they come seeking Him anyway.

In the passage above, Daniel not only confesses and grieves—
he also makes a bold request. He's saying, "Although we are
responsible for the breakdown in our relationship with you, we
are your people. We bear your name. We have not earned anything from you, and we are not in a place of deserving something
that we can demand from you. But please, do something. If not for
us, then at least for Your own sake—it has to be an embarrassment
to You that the people who belong to You in a special way are the
ones in ruin."

This is the kind of relationship that God invites us to have
with Him. We can ask for great things, even when we believe
that we have no reason to expect good things. Daniel felt that the
Word of God itself was saying "no deliverance" for seventy years
(see Dan. 9:2). But his response was to *ask anyway*. He saw the
devastation of sin, and he grieved, confessed, and asked boldly

for healing. This is a strong kind of hope—for Daniel, and for us today.

> **Reflect:** Is your "hope gauge" registering any activity? When do you notice it flagging?
>
> **Reflect:** Do you struggle with feeling unworthy to ask God for what is on your heart (e.g., forgiveness or reconciliation with family)?
>
> **Act:** Turn to the Lord and pray. Be honest about the messiness of your life—and then, even if you feel hopeless, ask for help. Let Daniel's prayer become your own: "God, please do something."

DAY 3

Knowing the Healer

When the teachers of the law who were Pharisees saw him
eating with the sinners and tax collectors, they asked his
disciples: "Why does he eat with tax collectors and sinners?"
On hearing this, Jesus said to them, "It is not the healthy
who need a doctor, but the sick. I have not come to call
the righteous, but sinners." (Mark 2:16–17 NIV)

MANY YEARS AGO, after I had been working the same tutoring job for a while, a coworker suggested that I ask for a raise. It was a great idea, I'm sure—but I didn't ask. I was embarrassed to ask. I had often been late filling out and turning in my time sheets. I wanted to look like I deserved the raise, so I felt like I needed to be better for a little while before asking.

Have you ever felt that impulse? It happens in many areas of life. People who are dealing with alcohol or sex addictions will always want a few days of being clean before admitting to someone that they've had a fall. They—and we—usually treat God the same way. We want a few days of being clean before we pray again. But the old hymn warns us, "If you tarry till you're better, you will never come at all."[1]

I believe that we hesitate because we have a hard time accepting that God is genuinely, meaningfully merciful. If you are like me, you will not want to come to God until you feel clean. But that's the very reason why we have to come to God. He is the one who will wash us and make us clean.

When Jesus wants to wash the disciples' feet, Peter protests, "No—I should be the one washing your feet." And Jesus says, "Unless you let me wash your feet, you have no part of me" (see John 13:6–8).[2] Jesus has to say it almost with harshness, because it is so important. Shame and embarrassment are that bad. They really could keep you from Jesus.

We can't shrink back in shame. But we do have to know that we're dirty and sick. Only then can we be cleaned and cured.

Going to the doctor makes sense only if you are not well. Jesus didn't come to help people who thought they had their act together and felt no sense of need. He came for the sick—for sinners who are coughing and dirty, who are walking into the ER without health insurance. "It is not the healthy who need a doctor, but the sick," Jesus says. And He calls the sick to the health of repentance. Who do sinners find pursuing them? This Great Physician is not a distant, sterile doctor in a white coat but one who is "not ashamed to call [us] brothers" (Heb. 2:11).

> **Reflect:** Have you started the conversation with God yet? If not, what kinds of things do you think are holding you back?
>
> **Reflect:** Are people telling you that you aren't taking things seriously enough or that you sound like you're minimizing or blame-shifting? Consider whether you feel yet that you need the Great Physician.

DAY 4

Keeping Pace

Let us also lay aside every weight, and sin which clings so closely,
and let us run with endurance the race that is set before us, looking
to Jesus, the founder and perfecter of our faith, who for the joy
that was set before him endured the cross. (Heb. 12:1–2)

I RECENTLY SIGNED up for my first race. It's only a 10K, but it's a hard run up and back down a small mountain. I have already started to notice that I don't pace myself well. And there is real danger of my not finishing (or at least not finishing well) if I run too hard early on. I have to go steady and build endurance one step at a time so that I avoid injury and (hopefully!) finish the race. Growing as a Christian is similar. It is never wrong to go hard and be as holy as you can, but there can be an intensity in the early stages of restoration that easily gives rise to unhelpful expectations. It's understandable—who wouldn't want to be done with all this as soon as possible?

But the call in Hebrews 12 is to run with endurance—to pace yourself for the long-distance race. What makes it possible to endure the whole way and make it home? Not your own strength, your ingenuity, or big symbolic actions—such as going to conferences, buying books, or joining groups (as helpful as those all can be). You look to "Jesus, the founder and perfecter of our faith" (v. 2). He gives you the strength, hope, and patience that you need to survive.

What gets in the way of endurance? All kinds of impatience. After all I am doing, why is my spouse not forgiving me yet? Why don't people see me as repentant yet? Why am I not back at home yet? Can't we put this behind us and move on? This impatience will entangle you (see v. 1) and weigh you down. It's dead weight,

23

and you want to run free. To avoid getting too weary, and to keep up our hope of finishing the race, we keep pace as we run and look to Jesus.

Reflect: Jesus "endured the cross, despising the shame" for you (Heb. 12:2). Keep your eyes focused on Him. Whatever this journey will look like for you, there will be many moments that feel like painful endurance. You will need Him.

Act: Take a moment to pray for pace. "Father, grant me patience—patience to admit the length of the journey ahead; patience to stay on the path; patience to hear the pain of others; patience to slow down, to learn, to grow, to change. Father, bring your restoration, bring smiles to the people I love, bring joy out of tears someday—but oh, please, someday soon. Help me, when I run, not to grow weary; when I walk, not to faint; and when I fall, to rise up on wings as eagles."

DAY 5

Sinners, Poor and Needy

Be sober-minded; be watchful. Your adversary the devil prowls around like a roaring lion, seeking someone to devour. (1 Peter 5:8)

BEING A SINNER in a fallen world always includes pain. Consider what afflicts you. How does our adversary assault and threaten to *devour* you?

The hymn says, "Come, ye sinners, poor and needy, weak and wounded, sick and sore."[1] These words paint a picture of a person suffering. You might expect the lyrics to say, "Come, you sufferers, oppressed and hurting." But it tells *sinners* to come. Sin is more than an affliction, but for Christians it is never less.

The sources of our greatest affliction are the world, the flesh, and the devil (see Eph. 2:1–3). They work together. The world tells us what sex is for, what we are entitled to, and so on. Its messages are persuasive. They come in big, direct ways, like the Ashley Madison slogan, "Life is Short. Have an Affair."[2] Its messages are subtler, too, such as movies suggesting that true love must overcome all barriers or that feelings must always be obeyed. Other times it's show-and-tell: "Look at this. Isn't it great? Don't you want it right now? Why not? Dive in!" These are assaults, and we should see them as trials and temptations—as afflictions from our adversary.[3]

Sin is not just something "out there," however. We ourselves are bent toward accepting these messages, and we even craft our own. *Go a little farther, then stop.* Or *Just this one time.* Sometimes the rationale is darker: *If I were connecting with my spouse, I wouldn't need this.* We say these things to coach ourselves past barriers, but at the core our inner demand is oriented toward the forbidden. It's so strong that it is willing to shortcut God's design. Or our distress and loneliness are so heavy that using another person to numb and distract ourselves feels like a good solution. This happens because we are fallen. We have the flesh at work within us (see Rom 7:18). And this is why the world's messages find such resonance in us.

But at this stage I, along with the hymn above (and with 1 Peter 5:8), am emphasizing the world's dangers—which we are often blind to. We live in a world of deception and affliction. We have been apprenticed, by the world around us, and well coached for adultery. We are in a threatening environment.

We are being hunted by a lion—the devil. We are in his territory, and he waits for just the right time to go for the kill. Infidelity is one of his favorite attacks. He sneaks up on us. We never think that it would happen to us. We don't really see it coming. And, by the time it's upon us, we were already in a very dangerous place. That's how effective he is.

He has wounded you. But he has not yet devoured you. So hear the warning of the One who wants to see you make it out alive—the One who knows the darkness well and knows how to overcome it: "Be sober-minded; be watchful." The lion is still on the hunt.

Reflect: How has the world around you taught you to view sex? How has it invited, coached, and apprenticed you to live?

Reflect: Which of the world's messages have you made your own?

Reflect: What messages did you create in order to get you past barriers?

Act: Ask God to be your refuge from the dangers you continue to face (see Ps. 46:1). Ask Him to forgive all your sins and heal all your diseases (see Ps. 103:3).

DAY 6

Satan's Plans

What I have forgiven, if I have forgiven anything, has been for your sake in the presence of Christ, so that we would not be outwitted by Satan; for we are not ignorant of his designs. (2 Cor. 2:10–11)

PAUL IS AWARE that we have a powerful adversary—one who has clear plans. The world around us has a clear pattern—a mindset that we are invited to adopt. We do not want to be "ignorant of his designs." The problem, though, is that we have internalized many of his deceptive messages and we play the game we've been coached to play. We have been "conformed to this world" (Rom. 12:2). That's part of why you may still miss the person who you had an affair with. It's part of why you find yourself critical, defensive, minimizing, and sometimes showing anger.

What are the adversary's plans? After infidelity, the best ways for him to keep you conformed to this world are:

- to keep you minimally aware of how you got where you did (but to keep you feeling assured that you know what you need to know about it).
- to keep you from being aware of the damage that infidelity causes (but to persuade you that, truly, you do already know).
- to keep you talking about how things are getting better (rather than dealing with the constructive criticism you're hearing).
- to keep you assured that you have all the help you need (and that you don't need to bring a friend, pastor, or counselor into the loop).

All these plans and schemes are ways for you to be "conformed to this world." The world doesn't care much about the humility that it takes to receive criticism well. The world assures us that we are uniquely capable at most things, and certainly that we don't need others in order to achieve our goals. It teaches a confidence that is rooted not in the calm assurance of the will of God (Rom. 12:2) but in ourselves.

The patterns of this world are ugly. Satan loves to outwit people. Join the Lord in humble but righteous anger over everything that leads His precious ones astray. You, too, are one of His precious ones. He does not want to see you led astray.

Reflect: What are the adversary's plans for you? In what ways has he outwitted you?

Act: Pray. "Most holy God, the source of all good desires, all right judgments, and all just works: Give to us, your servants, that peace which the world cannot give, so that our minds may be fixed on the doing of your will, and that we, being delivered from the fear of all enemies, may live in peace and quietness; through the mercies of Christ Jesus our Savior. Amen."[1]

Act: Write down a few notes in answer to this question: What is God's will for me today? This week? This month?

DAY 7

Making Urgency Good

Hear my prayer, O LORD; give ear to my pleas for mercy!
In your faithfulness answer me, in your righteousness! . . . Answer
me quickly, O LORD! My spirit fails! . . . Deliver me from my
enemies, O LORD! I have fled to you for refuge. Teach me to
do your will, for you are my God! . . . In your righteousness
bring my soul out of trouble! (Ps. 143:1, 7, 9–10, 11)

SO FAR YOU have begun to grieve and to say, "The enemy has pursued my soul" (Ps. 143:3). Maybe you are also quicker to say, "Deliver me from my enemies, O LORD!" (v. 9). You feel now that the world around you is dangerous. Maybe you have stopped going certain places, cut off certain friendships, taken indefinite breaks from some forms of media. People start to do this when they feel urgency.

Do you hear the urgency of the psalmist? The exclamation points, the intense words, the pleading. He's in a place of darkness and despair. The enemy has crushed his life to the ground (see v. 3). You might feel some of this same urgency. You want things to be better. You hate the place that you're in.

The trouble is that expressing this urgency in most of your relationships won't be very helpful. Your spouse, your kids, your friends, and your church leaders all need to see a quiet, dedicated, well-paced walk forward. They won't find it easy to trust what might look or feel like a quick fix. You yourself may feel assured that a renewed devotional, a support group, or a moment of surrender has dealt a decisive blow to your sexual sin—but that no actions you take are enough to assure others and rebuild their trust. It will be difficult for you to take it slowly. Any delay or misunderstanding will feel consequential. You fear that things will go poorly for you if people don't see that you've changed—and fast. Hence the urgency.

Let all that urgency funnel into your prayers. Your spouse may not be able to believe your passionate promises that things have changed. But God is able and eager to hear your angst and passion, and he will refine it and channel it into action.

Toward the end of the book of Psalms, Israel grows increasingly hopeless that God will send a righteous king to make things right. "No one living is righteous before you" (Ps. 143:2). So they start asking God to do it Himself—asking that He would be their King and Deliverer. "In your righteousness bring my soul out of trouble!" (v. 11). Allow yourself to despair of the possibility of figuring things out and setting them right quickly. This will be terrifying. It will feel like you're losing what little control you had. But this process is necessarily slow. You have urgent needs, but your most urgent need is to wait on the Lord and to quietly, faithfully take the first steps forward.

Reflect: Prayer is a good way to shift toward the right kind of urgency. The wrong kind of urgency is a personal striving and scheming to fix things. To pray is to admit that you yourself cannot fix things. Prayer shows a dependence on God to change your heart and your spouse's heart. Where are you finding an unhelpful urgency, rushing, or franticness in your thoughts, words, or actions?

Act: Rather than rushing, channel your passion and angst into prayer. God is eager to hear your requests.

DAY 8

Afflicted but Not Afflicting

*"In your anger do not sin": Do not let the sun go down while
you are still angry, and do not give the devil a foothold. Anyone
who has been stealing must steal no longer, but must work, doing
something useful with their own hands, that they may have
something to share with those in need. (Eph. 4:26–28 NIV)*

IN VIEW OF the forces that are waging war against every Christian, it makes sense to be angry. We have a real enemy. But "in your anger do not sin"; rather, speak the truth and work with a view toward service and love. If we fail in this, our adversary gains a foothold. One key problem for you to avoid is directing anger or frustration at your spouse in this season. It may be very difficult at times. You will get the heat. You will feel afflicted. No one is happy with you.

Your spouse will need lots of grace as well as space to feel complex and conflicting emotions. He or she may not respond to you with patience, grace, and gentleness for the indefinite future.

The old self was the way not of patience and grace but of "deceitful desires" (Eph. 4:22). The new self, though, is the one trained by Christ (see vv. 21, 23–24). How do we learn from Him? Like Him, expect to feel unfairly treated. Unlike Him, expect to feel resentment and self-centered anger. Like Him, "in your anger do not sin." Slow down. Like Him, seek to speak truthfully and in love. Aim for plain, honest communication, because "we are all members of one body" (v. 25 NIV). Offer more than words, too. Take restorative action. What your past actions have taken away, seek to restore. Seek to work hard and be useful, focusing on the work of your hands and sharing whatever extra you have (see v. 28). At very least, this means slowing

31

down and doing the work in front of you each day, both in and out of the house.

> **Reflect:** What are potential areas where the adversary could gain a foothold in you? Are you frustrated with your spouse?
>
> **Reflect:** What restorative actions are available to you? Is your family willing to receive these yet, or are you in a season of waiting?
>
> **Act:** Look at the last paragraph of today's reading, and find a way to be like Christ in showing love to your spouse today. In your next conversation together, can you speak truthfully and in love, plainly and honestly? And can you offer more than words? Can you initiate a restorative action, work hard, and be useful?

DAY 9

Friends for the Journey

*Brothers and sisters, if someone is caught in a sin, you who live by
the Spirit should restore that person gently. But watch yourselves,
or you also may be tempted. Carry each other's burdens, and in
this way you will fulfill the law of Christ. (Gal. 6:1–2 NIV)*

AT TIMES YOU will feel the pressure to limit the circle of those
who know what has happened. There's some wisdom in that—
certainly not everyone needs to know everything. Be careful not
to cut off sources of care, though. There is no way to be restored
alone. In order to select people who can help you, look for people
who fit Paul's description in these verses, and welcome their
input. Do you have a friend who can be gentle and humble? Will
this friend tell you the uncomfortable truth? Does this friend
walk by the Spirit? Does he or she carry burdens? Ask these questions, but don't over-evaluate friends and helpers. Reach out.

Who in church leadership do you feel most comfortable talking with? What are your hesitations? Let me encourage you to err
on the side of seeking their help, even if you find yourself thinking, *Well, he doesn't have time for me—he's more of an administrator
and preacher than a caretaker.* Give your pastor the chance.

Your spouse will also need people to talk with. This may feel
threatening. *What will be said when I am not in the room? Who
will those people talk to? Will people gossip and spread rumors?* Do
your best to free your spouse of any feeling of needing to hide
things and suffer in silence. You and your spouse will grow best
in the light.

One of the surprises of God's grace is that you yourself
should soon become a person who walks in the Spirit and can
then carry burdens as well. This is a key piece of the transition

from controlling to caretaking—from being a person who does damage control and shuts down uncomfortable feedback to being a person who cares for others.[1] Your spouse has heavy burdens in this season. How will you become a person who cares for your spouse? Observe and study: what does your spouse need? Bearing burdens in this way will mean listening without defensiveness, affirming and validating, removing all sense of criticism and pressure, initiating hard conversations. This is relieving for someone who is carrying a burden.

Hang onto this idea of a "burden." What is heavy for your spouse? Can you carry it? Begin to think about what the impact of your actions has been. What burden did your actions create?

Carrying burdens fulfills "the law of Christ." What is Christ's law? Love of God and neighbor. This love is patient, kind, not demanding, and not irritable, but deeply hopeful (see 1 Cor. 13). God gives us this love.

> **Reflect:** What heavy burden can you bear for your spouse? What small burdens can you carry to lighten your spouse's load in this season?
>
> **Act:** Consider who might bear your burdens with you in this season. Make a list of your support team. Consider including a pastor/elder, a counselor, and at least two friends. Talk with them, and decide together how frequently you will maintain contact and what they will anticipate providing for you.

DAY 10

Discovering Resentment

*Human anger does not produce the righteousness
that God desires. (James 1:20 NIV)*

YOU ARE WELL aware of your spouse's flaws, and perhaps
they are even more apparent to you in this moment. I have never
seen someone who has been unfaithful who did not also struggle
with anger or resentment during the restoration process. That's
because resentment makes infidelity possible, and it tends to
linger on.

The starting point of an affair is typically some sort of pain:
loneliness, feeling wronged or ignored, distance, lack of affirmation, boredom, numbness, lack of vitality, loss of direction or
identity. Yet none of these leads straight to adultery. There is an
intermediate step: resentment. *I was wronged; it was unfair; I am
angry about it*. It can be resentment toward a spouse, but it can
also be resentment toward parents, a boss, and even God. We tell
a narrative of mistreatment, we feel that we deserve better, and we
take it into our own hands.

This mindset doesn't end when the affair ends. Knee-jerk
resentment and criticism typically remain for a long time after-
ward. Let me invite you to adopt a very difficult principle for this
season: give no criticism to your spouse. It is certainly possible
that the affair happened in direct connection with how you felt
about some of what your spouse was doing or not doing. You
had real concerns. But the worst that your spouse was able to do
was to contribute to conditions that made your faithfulness more
difficult. Nothing justifies infidelity. I doubt that you would say
so. But the mitigating circumstances still seem relevant to talk
about, don't they? They seem to come up so easily.

If you want to share blame, then by all means do so—just not with your spouse. Remember that the world tutors us away from Christian faithfulness. Remember that the adversary is a lion who hunts and devours. When it comes to your spouse, seek wisdom by holding back criticism. "A fool gives full vent to his spirit, but a wise man quietly holds it back" (Prov. 29:11). Feelings of anger and entitlement after pain—i.e., resentment—do not produce the right living that God requires. Anger promises to right wrongs and ensure fairness. But it is powerless to bring about the true justice of God (see James 1:20). You must be ruthless in self-control, in restraint, in enduring the unpleasant feelings.

At a later time, when the key elements of healing from the affair have happened, you will have the opportunity for marriage counseling that is more mutual, when you will be free to share about the new kind of marriage that you want and about the pains of the old way of relating. But that becomes fruitful only after the hard work of healing from the affair. If you introduce constructive criticism too early, it can too easily be overcome and twisted by feelings of resentment.

> **Reflect:** Where do you see yourself feeling resentful? What is the pain underneath your resentment? How do you see God coming close to provide comfort?
>
> **Act:** Turn to your support network (your pastor, counselor, or mentors) and ask them to help you sort through your resentment. Ask for space to talk it through, and for feedback and perspective. Don't bottle it all up, even though you know that it's ugly. A wise friend can handle it and help; and, more than that, God Himself loves to be with His children and is very generous to their requests for help (see Matt. 7:9–11).

DAY 11

Trust the Process

*Obey your leaders and submit to them, for they are keeping
watch over your souls, as those who will have to give an
account. Let them do this with joy and not with groaning, for
that would be of no advantage to you. (Heb. 13:17)*

THE MINDSET OF adultery does not welcome direction or
redirection from others—and especially not from leaders. It will
make sure to remind you that not all leaders are wise or helpful
(see Ezek. 34).[1] But do not assume that destructive leadership
will be the norm. Invite the help of caring church leadership.

After adultery, proactive church leaders step in to provide
structure and expectations as part of the church discipline process or as guidelines for avoiding church discipline. You will likely
face temptation to edit or shorten the process they lay out. The
command in Hebrews to follow godly leadership is there because
there is a real temptation not to.

I encourage you to fully engage with the restoration plan
and also *not* to dictate and control the process. Releasing hyper-
independence and control is part of living in community and
being cared for by wise shepherds. More than that, we belong to
Jesus, our Good Shepherd; and through His church He helps us
when we stray. Let it be a relief, not a burden—it is not all up
to us, or all in our control, to fix things. When leaders help you
to outline a process for restoration, trust the process.

For several years, the Philadelphia 76ers picked an unusual
strategy for revamping their basketball team. The idea was, in
effect, to lose a lot of games *on purpose* for a few years, and then to
be first in line to get top draft picks every year. "Trust the process,"
they told the fans. But there comes a time when losses get to be

too many. Fans get angry. Tickets don't sell. People get fired. It's hard to be patient with the process.

You've probably heard stories of famous pastors who had affairs and then began a process of restoration, only to pull out a few months in. Sadly, this is common. It is hard to trust a long and painful process, and hard to trust God in the process.

Let me recommend what may sound like two oxymorons: engaged compliance and flexible commitment. Some people accept a recommended recovery plan with no complaints. But if you had no role in crafting the plan, or no buy-in on the reasons for the plan's components, you will soon grow resentful and exasperated with it.[2] If you are compliant, remain *engaged*.

Others are fully committed and take decisive action. They make their plan—so far so good. The problem is that most of us don't know what we need. We don't have the insight that we will have later. So we must be flexible and be active in getting feedback. If you are committed, stay *flexible*. In view of Hebrews 13, when you receive wise plans from caring leaders, give your obedience and submission actively.

Reflect: Do you feel willing to trust the process? What holds you back? How do you see God at work in the (imperfect) process that your leaders have recommended?

Act: What is your plan? If you don't have one yet, start writing the key elements that you think you should include. Then take it to others and get their input. Sample categories to consider: media restrictions, transparency commitments, regular meetings with various helpers, and more.

COMING CLEAN TO GOD AND OTHERS

As you come to God in confession and repentance, you also learn to move toward your spouse. Learning to apologize requires wrestling with the impact of your actions on others and fully (but lovingly) disclosing what has happened. Confession and asking for forgiveness are not one-time actions but are typically the fruit of a process of humble listening and reflection.

DAY 12

Learning How to Apologize

Our sins are piled up before God and testify against us. . . .
We know we have rebelled and have denied the LORD.
We have turned our backs on our God. We know how
unfair and oppressive we have been, carefully planning
our deceitful lies. (Isa. 59:12, 13–14 NLT)

IT FEELS SO shocking to be in a broken place after falling hard. But if you start to look, you will find many small steps that led you to where you are now. Today's passage invites us to confess "carefully planning our deceitful lies" (v. 14). As hard as it is not to look away, consider your actions.

You may find yourself saying, "Believe me, I know what I've done." Yet the reality is that none of us does. If we did, the full weight of what we've done wrong would crush us. But the more we grow as Christians, the more we see both the depth of our sin and the greatness of the cross in covering it—even in the shameful details.

Someone once told me that he didn't know how to apologize. "I mean, what can you say after 'I'm sorry'?" As we were talking, however, we realized that his apologies were comprised of about 5 percent actual apology ("I'm really, really sorry") and 95 percent explanation of mitigating circumstances ("Here's what else was happening"; "Here's what you did that was so frustrating"; and so on).

He said that he didn't want to shift blame or be defensive and that he wanted to learn how to apologize. I was so glad that he asked. Christians have had to work at doing this well for a very long time. Here is one example:

Almighty and most merciful Father,

>   we have erred and strayed from your ways like lost sheep.
>   we have followed too much the deceits and desires of our
>   own hearts.
>   we have offended against your holy laws.
>   we have left undone those things which we ought to
>   have done,
>   and we have done those things which we ought not to
>   have done;
>   and apart from your grace, there is no health in us.

O Lord, have mercy upon us.

>   Spare all those who confess their faults.
>   Restore those who are penitent, according to your promises
>   declared
>   to all people in Christ Jesus our Lord;
> And grant, O most merciful Father, for his sake,
>   that we may now live a godly, righteous, and sober life,
>   to the glory of your holy Name. Amen.[1]

This prayer is directed to God. Sin is first an offense against Him: "our sins are piled up before God . . . we have rebelled and have denied the LORD" (Is. 59:12–13). This prayer, like David's in Psalm 51 (which we will explore on day 16), has general elements but invites specificity. *What did I do? What did I leave undone? Where was my deceit? What were the desires I followed?* Naming them to the Lord prepares us to speak to others about them in order to restore relationships.

> **Reflect:** Consider what prepared the way for your adultery— what patterns of sin (share your sexual history with a helper) and what attitudes or dispositions (consider things such as selfishness, presumption, entitlement). Speak to God about this.

DAY 13

Intent vs. Impact

*Do not be deceived: God is not mocked, for whatever
one sows, that will he also reap. (Gal. 6:7)*

ONCE, WHEN I WAS A KID, I was watching my dad help
some men to move the pulpit at our church in order to clear the
stage for the play he was in that evening. The pulpit tipped on the
dolly and fell on my dad's toe. I thought it was hilarious at first,
like something out of the Three Stooges. He didn't enjoy it. He
had to go to the hospital, and it turned out that he could barely
get medicated enough to make it through the play walking on a
broken toe.

You can imagine that I felt pretty bad about my initial reac-
tion. Neither I nor the men helping to move the pulpit had
intended any harm, but there was *impact*.

Do you remember your intentions before the infidelity?
Many people just want to be a friendly coworker, a listening
ear, an encouraging presence. Sometimes the intent is clear: *I'm
unhappy and I want out.* For some, their marriage felt hopeless in
an ultimate way. *It was either suicide or this.* Desire for self-harm
is not sound rationale for major life decisions, but those kinds of
statements aren't uncommon, and they speak to a great depth of
pain and a great desire for relief. The intention, they might say,
was not to hurt their spouse but to stop their own hurt.

Your intentions matter. Infidelity is worse if you intend harm.
But the impact can be the same, whether or not that impact was
intended. Believe it or not, God (and your spouse) does care
about the *intent* of your actions. But both are also very interested
in the *impact* of your actions.

We often do not have an accurate picture of the impact or

seriousness of our actions. The rich young ruler did not have an accurate handle on the seriousness of his problem. The solution that Jesus offered seemed overly severe to him—preposterously severe—because he was blind to the true nature of his problem. *How could I really need to give up everything I own?*

Much of the Bible's moral framework operates on the principle of sowing and reaping (see Gal. 6:7)—the seed that you put in the ground brings a harvest later on. Regardless of intention, if infidelity is planted, it brings a devastating harvest. It impacts you and others on a surprising scale. How could a small seed create such a big tree? How could one action lead to all this?

Some consequences are more immediate: the hurt and pain of your spouse, the harm to your marriage. Some are long-term: the unrepentant adulterer will not inherit the kingdom of God (see 1 Cor. 6:9–10).

We have to take seriously the ways we have impacted others, regardless of our intentions.

Reflect: What impact have your actions had on your spouse, children, and church? How have they hurt these relationships? What has been the fallout?

Act: Start a process of learning the impact that your actions have had.[1] (1) Answer the reflection questions above. (2) Share your answers with a friend, counselor, or pastor, and receive their feedback. (3) Reflect more and revise your idea of the impact based on their feedback. (4) Share with your spouse your idea of the impact you have caused, and receive feedback. Continue to reflect and revise, cycling through steps 1–4.

Not Pulling the Rug Out from under Your Spouse

For when I kept silent, my bones wasted away through my groaning all day long. For day and night your hand was heavy upon me; my strength was dried up as by the heat of summer. I acknowledged my sin to you, and I did not cover my iniquity; I said, "I will confess my transgressions to the LORD," and you forgave the iniquity of my sin. (Ps. 32:3–5)

PSALM 32 TELLS US that confession starts with acknowledging our sin to the Lord. Instead of keeping silent (v. 3) or covering up sin (v. 5a), you must go to Him, confess, and seek forgiveness (v. 5b). Silence and hiding are deadly for relationships. The God who sees all already knows what we have done. But He is far from us when we are dishonest and unrepentant. And what we do in our relationship with the Lord has a great impact on all of our relationships. We aren't supposed to bring a gift to the altar unless we have made things right with others (see Matt. 5:24). Confession is always twofold—to God and to others (see James 5:16).

Early full disclosure to your spouse is vital, because if significant details come out later, your spouse will feel that the wound has been reopened, and this will delay the process of rebuilding trust. People often delay confession until things are better. It's for a good reason—they say that they don't want to cause their spouse more pain. I promise you that this is not how it will go. The longer the time under the lie, the harder it will be to rebuild the marriage. Many spouses say that it is not so much the sexual or even emotional elements of affairs that are most damaging. It is the deception.

I am pleading with you to come clean, accept the risk of oversharing, and confess sooner rather than later. If it comes out later, betrayed spouses feel like the rug has been pulled out from under them.

It is also important not to confess impulsively. It can bring tremendous relief to come clean in a climactic moment when you can bear the secrecy no more. But pay attention to your spouse. As a rule, confessing over a text message or phone call, or sharing comments on the way out the door or before your child's concert, are not loving or considerate ways to disclose.[1]

Also, avoid sharing details that create a strong visual picture or image. Spouses do need to know key events, but sharing vivid detail can create unnecessary pain. Even so, many spouses would say that they would rather know more than know less.

What I am asking of you will feel like death. But I promise you it will be spiritual life and health. If Psalm 32 is a picture of wasting away in silence, it is also a picture of finding a lasting safe place in God Himself and being surrounded with shouts of deliverance. Can you imagine the battle cry—the loud cheering that God is here to help, to rescue, to bring you to safety? The incentive to come clean is powerful—it is the path toward walking closely with Him, surrounded by His steadfast love (see v. 10).

Reflect: What is preventing you from full disclosure? What reasons and arguments in your mind are holding you back?

Act: When you are preparing to confess more fully to your spouse, it can be one of the scariest moments of your life. Consider how God is offering you a hiding place (see Ps. 32:7–8) and what He is putting in your life to preserve you. Look for His care.

DAY 15

Not Sweeping Things
under the Rug

*God is light, and in him is no darkness at all. If we say we have
fellowship with him while we walk in darkness, we lie and do
not practice the truth. But if we walk in the light, as he is in
the light, we have fellowship with one another, and the blood
of Jesus his Son cleanses us from all sin. (1 John 1:5–7)*

IT IS ALMOST certain that you will want to move quickly past discussion of painful past events (who wouldn't want to?). Let me urge you not to, as painful as this will be. God is shining His light into a very dark place (your heart and mine, continually), and the brightness stings. But we are not merely to step into the light at one point and time—we are to learn to *live* there. This means humble admissions. Nothing to hide and nothing to rush past, because God's grace grants us a profound security.

Walking in the light leads to two great benefits. First, *we have fellowship with one another* (see 1 John 1:7a). If you are feeling isolated and misunderstood, you might think that exposure would only increase this. Why add more embarrassment? But walking in the light actually connects you with others—and especially with your spouse. It is your best hope of regaining closeness. Second, *the blood of Jesus cleanses us from all sin* (see v. 7b). You are probably sick of feeling dirty. Being honest is exposing, but it makes you clean. If you've missed having a sense of integrity and self-respect, this is the most direct path to having a clear conscience before God.

Here are elements you will want to consider bringing into the light.

- *The offense.* Simple enough—speak plainly about what you did. Use clear language, without either vagueness or lurid detail.
- *What else happened.* Affairs are never isolated events. What else did you do around this time? Start by discussing your sexual history with your pastor, counselor, or trusted friend. Don't leave anything out. Thoroughness of events, without lurid detail, is best. Make a timeline. Discuss how you will share these things with your spouse—again avoiding both bland generality and unnecessary detail. It will be important for him or her to know what has happened, and on the sooner side. You will not want your spouse to begin to feel that things have stabilized, only to discover more information later and feel that the rug has been pulled out from under him or her. Consider including the "ways of escape" you passed over and the summary of what else you did. Admit to paying attention to people who should have received professional distance, to flirting, to phone calls, to fantasy, to planning, to lying.
- *Attitudes.* An affair always includes dispositions and habits of mind. Consider topics such as presumption, self-orientedness, and entitlement. What did you tell yourself in order to feel better about what you were doing? How did you make it okay in your mind?

Reflect: As you confess your sin and step into the light, know that God's mercy waits for you on the other end. "Whoever conceals his transgressions will not prosper, but he who confesses and forsakes them will obtain mercy" (Prov. 28:13). Does that give you further incentive to come clean?

Act: Disclose the elements that are recommended above in a safe context with a counselor, pastor, or support group.

DAY 16

Confessing Well

I know my transgressions, and my sin is ever before me. Against you, you only, have I sinned and done what is evil in your sight, so that you may be justified in your words and blameless in your judgment. . . . Purge me with hyssop, and I shall be clean; wash me, and I shall be whiter than snow. (Ps. 51:3–4, 7)

PSALM 51 MAKES it clear: sin is ugly, and repentance requires feelings as well as words and actions. External influences and circumstances are treated as relevant but are not emphasized. Consequences are seen as just and fair, even merciful. The tone is humble. God's mercy is predominant.

You've probably already said you were sorry. That was a vital step. But confession and repentance are not one-time acts—they are a shape of the Christian life. Martin Luther said, "Our Lord and Master Jesus Christ . . . intended that the whole life of believers should be penitence."[1]

Confession includes both an initial decision and an ongoing effort—an initial act of honesty and an ongoing pursuit of honesty. This is not to say you will wear sackcloth and ashes for the next twenty years. But the *turning* of repentance requires a process of course correction. You've turned on to the right road, but you're not yet driving within the lines.

Confessing well requires listening well. You will need to become a student of your spouse's (and family's) experience of you pre-affair.[2] You will likely find that you've been self-centered and unloving in other areas.[3] That will be very painful. It will require massive amounts of patience and humility. But it is essential for a meaningful confession.

The reason that thoroughness is so vital is that the sin was not just in the act but in many small acts before, during, and after it. At some point in the future, it will be fine to summarize the events broadly, but not before you face up to the specifics of what you are confessing.

Marriage vows commit us to stay with our spouses through a list of possible circumstances—the idea is that no one should get through the wedding without knowing what you've gotten yourself into. Confession to your spouse is similar to this. You need to know what you're asking the person to forgive you for, and not just in general terms. Betrayed spouses already know what they are signing up for by staying in the marriage—and they usually know this with a good deal of clarity. But it is vital that *you* know what they are signing up for. This will foster appreciation and gentleness. And then you'll experience what we all *want* to feel toward our spouses: that we don't deserve how good we have it.

Many people feel ready to confess generally: *Don't you realize that every day I regret that I blew up my marriage and ruined everything?* That won't take us far enough, though. As the Westminster Confession says, "It is every man's duty to endeavor to repent of his particular sins particularly."[4] We must admit specifically to specific sins if we want to truly repent.

Reflect: What do you need to confess specifically?

Act: Write out a detailed confession (e.g., "Here is what I have done, and here is what I ought to have done. I have offended you in this way," etc.). You will find it initially discouraging, but pray through it and add a note of God's forgiveness and mercy at the end. If a counselor or pastor thinks you are ready, talk to your spouse about these things in a safe context. This a scary but necessary step. Remember that full disclosure will be important to reconciling.

BUILDING A TESTIMONY

Sin is chaotic, disordered, and confusing. It doesn't initially fit into the storyline of a believer's life—it is out of place and is hard to make sense of. But forgiven sinners have stories to tell. God weaves each person's story into a testimony.

Our task is not just to avoid writing ourselves in as the hero. We are biased storytellers, and we don't see ourselves clearly. So we need to release control of the story. A testimony of *God's* work requires humility. This humility frees us to take a sober look at the depths of our hearts, and then we find that God's redeeming love goes deeper still. All this makes for a powerful story of grace.

DAY 17

God's Narrative

For the love of Christ controls us, because we have concluded this:
that one has died for all, therefore all have died; and he died for
all, that those who live might no longer live for themselves but for
him who for their sake died and was raised. (2 Cor. 5:14–15)

THE BIBLE OFTEN speaks of wisdom with great nuance. Other times wisdom is laid out as a choice between two clear alternatives: "Do nothing out of selfish ambition or vain conceit. Rather, in humility value others above yourselves, not looking to your own interests but each of you to the interests of the others" (Phil. 2:3–4 NIV).

In this season, your urge to clarify will be overwhelming. We compulsively defend ourselves. But it is vital that you release control of the narrative and put the interests of your spouse first.

This has practical value. As Shirley Glass says, "The person who is betrayed rarely appreciates the subtleties."[1] *But we only did this, not that!* just doesn't make things better. You may try to control the details of the story out of the belief that it will be better for your spouse. But let the love of Christ compel you (see 2 Cor. 5:14) not to exasperate your spouse with subtleties. I'm glad that nothing happened that is worse than what did happen. And, yes, some clarifications matter. But don't fight for every detail.

It goes like this. Your spouse says, "You were planning all along, as soon as I left town. You must think I am so stupid." The reality is usually more complex, but this isn't the time to clarify details. Go for being brief while staying engaged through the pain. For example, phrases like "What I have done is awful, and I was not thinking of you as I should have or considering the pain this would cause" will *invite connection* rather than posture you to fight.

Your spouse will sometimes get the details sloppy, exaggerate, or get part of the story wrong. Everything in you will zero in on the incorrect detail rather than on the substance of what your spouse has said. Remember that your spouse's harsh words often indicate overwhelming pain, not a request to litigate the details. *If you want to heal your relationship with your spouse, you will have to let go of control of the narrative.* You will want to hear the story told a certain way that assigns just the right amount of the blame to yourself, and not any more. Totally understandable. But I promise you that if you take much time trying to control the story, you will lose chances to have healing conversations.

What controls you? It is the love of Christ that must control—not fear, not the desire to get every detail right, not the demand to hear the story told your way. What frees you? We don't live to ourselves when we know that we belong to Jesus, since He died for us and was raised. This was part of the reason Jesus died and rose—it was with a view toward His people living for Him, and not to themselves. He "gave himself for us to redeem us from all lawlessness and to purify for himself a people for his own possession who are zealous for good works" (Titus 2:14).

Reflect: Where are you having unnecessary conflicts? Where do you find yourself being defensive or counterattacking? What are your spouse's interests? How can you place them above your own?

Act: Remember that God is sovereign over your situation (see Isa. 40:21–26). Ask the Lord to help you let go of your control of the narrative. Trust him with the details.

DAY 18

Wearing Humility

Clothe yourselves, all of you, with humility toward one another,
for "God opposes the proud but gives grace to the humble."
Humble yourselves, therefore, under the mighty hand of God
so that at the proper time he may exalt you, casting all your
anxieties on him, because he cares for you. (1 Peter 5:5–7)

I'M NOT SURE that people ever think of themselves as proud. In times when our wrongs are clear, it's easy for us to feel that we've been as low as a person could go. But it's surprisingly hard to be truly humble after a fall. At the very least, what you say may not *sound* humble to other people for a long time. *But how do they know my heart? Who are they to accuse? Only God knows whether I have humbled myself!* Hear me out. The perspective that makes adultery possible prevents humility from growing during that time. To enjoy what is forbidden is to act out of entitlement, whether or not it's deliberate or even conscious. You may be disciplined, generous, and hardworking in much of your life. There may be almost nothing else about you that a person could look at and call it entitled—how you handle your job and how you handle money may be of the highest integrity. Thank the Lord for this. But at least in one area, a sense of entitlement has had room to grow. The perspective that infidelity requires, the perspective of entitlement, makes humility impossible—temporarily.

So it is vital for you to start the process of humility. Built into growth in humility is patience—God's blessing from humility comes only, as Peter points out, *in due time.* Godly, faithful character is built over time. So I invite you to start with this approach: Don't ask, "Am I humble?" Ask, "Where is pride getting through my defenses?" You're working hard, and that's good. But we're not expecting perfection—we're anticipating that God will continue to give us a lamp for our feet and a light for our path, showing us what He calls us to next. And that requires seeing where He is changing us next—the places where pride breaks through the defenses.

As you fight pride, strive for humility. Peter's command is to "clothe yourselves . . . with humility toward one another" (1 Peter 5:5). Put it on like your work clothes. It will prepare you well for the day and suit you for the tasks at hand. The reward promised for humility is the exact opposite of what you experience when you are exposed in infidelity: "Humble yourselves . . . so that at the proper time he may exalt you" (v. 6). It is frightening to release defensiveness and minimization. *What if people assume the worst?* Peter answers, "[Cast] all your anxieties on him, because he cares for you" (v. 7)

Act: Write out the story of what happened, underlining any places where you talk about anything bad that anyone else has done, or about mitigating factors (such as intensity of the temptation, extenuating circumstances, or good intentions).

Act: Cross out the underlined sections. That information is relevant, but not for the task of humility.

Act: Try reading the story again, out loud, without the wrongs of others and mitigating factors. Pay attention to the feeling of wanting to add extra comments when this shortened story puts a negative cast on you. Sit with the feeling, and let it pass. Endure it with the Lord—He knows the full backstory, and He has compassion toward our weakness. But right now He invites you to the difficult path of humility.

DAY 19

Learning What
Responsibility Means

*For we will all stand before the judgment seat of God; for it is
written, "As I live, says the Lord, every knee shall bow to me,
and every tongue shall confess to God." So then each of us will
give an account of himself to God. (Rom. 14:10–12)*

THERE IS NO question that a trap is set for people who are
seeking to follow Christ. The world around us is active in setting
the trap—active in seducing, active in misleading, active in shap-
ing unhelpful expectations. Yesterday I invited you to walk the
difficult path to humility and to face the ugliness of pride. Now
I want to invite you to take a step further into the thorny issue
of taking responsibility. It is complicated, because I've never met
people who do not think that they already take full responsibility.

Here is a test you can give yourself to start: *At this moment,
am I more aware of the ways I have been wronged or of the ways I
have wronged others?* Let Romans 14 resound in our ears whenever our focus veers to the failings of others, so that we say to
ourselves, *I will give account for myself to God. Let my own actions
be my concern.* To this end, you'll find it helpful to use "I" and
"my" statements as often as you can. Sometimes "we," "us," and
"our" can be helpful as well—but not yet "you" and "your."

Remember the exercise from yesterday, and start to express
your storyline in this new way to the helpers (the pastor, counselor, and friends) in your life. This new way emphasizes your own
agency, your own responsibility. It is hard at first, but it is a place
of real strength to know that you are accepting full responsibility.
Try speaking plainly about yourself as the person who has fallen,

without qualifications. If you believe, deeply, that you alone are to blame for what has happened, you will speak humbly and graciously. I promise you that it will be a breath of fresh air to people listening. It does not ensure that people will treat you well or affirm your progress, but it will be a testament to God's work. It will ultimately be deeply hope-giving for you to affirm your own sense of agency, because this is the precursor to experiencing the forgiving, healing love of God. Knowing yourself as you really are opens the door to experiencing God as He really is. *I am one who bows and confesses and gives account; He is my Judge, so I answer to Him.*

Reflect: Are there particular hurts that seem to dominate your thoughts? Do the hurts center on a particular person or event?

Reflect: Is anyone telling you that you are acting as though you are a victim? Is this a fair criticism?

Act: Ask a friend or counselor whether anything you have said gave the impression that you feel you are the more offended or aggrieved party. Welcome this feedback, and do your best not to fight it. If it is helpful, go back to the story that you wrote out yesterday (day 18) and edit it based on today's feedback. The circumstances of the affair are relevant, but not for the task of owning your sense of agency. You want to meaningfully convey your belief that the affair is your fault. You are not the sole reason for general tension in the marriage, since that is nearly always a two-way street. But no one is forced into an affair, since it comes not from circumstances but from the heart (see Matt. 15:19).

DAY 20

Out of the Heart

*"For out of the heart come evil thoughts, murder, adultery, sexual
immorality, theft, false witness, slander." (Matt. 15:19)*

I KNOW THAT the marriage wasn't perfect. I know that your
spouse wasn't, either. Systemic forces were at work in what happened. Some distance emerged. Some faults were never healed.
Clearly you perceived some problem in the "us" long ago. All
marriages have times that could serve as occasions for stepping
outside the marriage. Every marriage has moments of distance,
disappointment, fear, and complication.

Although sexual sin never happens outside the influence of
a broken world, Jesus makes a fascinating statement: ultimately,
adultery comes from the heart.

In the Bible, the heart is the core of who you are (see Prov.
20:5; Luke 6:43–45). The heart generates thoughts, desires, and
motives. It is the command center—out of your heart comes
your life.

If adultery comes from the heart, then it did not ultimately
come from your marriage. Responsibility is to be owned com-
pletely and personally. Bearing the blame may feel overwhelming or hopeless at first, but it is actually the beginning of hope.
If you have to wait for others to fix their contribution to what
happened, you are trapped. Accepting blame for the affair opens
the door for changing. And it is often disarming to people around
you. Other people will be harshest on you if it sounds like you are
blaming your spouse.

If the reasons for an affair are largely in the circumstances,
there is no hope that the circumstances will not overtake you
again. But if it really comes from your heart, then there is

hope—because changing the heart is exactly what God loves to do. "I will give you a new heart and put a new spirit in you; I will remove from you your heart of stone and give you a heart of flesh" (Ezek. 36:26 NIV).

Remember day 19 briefly. Strengthening your own sense of agency initially takes you away from emphasizing problems in the marriage. If *I* did it, then I am more concerned about the problems in me than about the problems in my marriage. But, paradoxically, personal agency is the path to mutuality. The ability to self-critique—to own blame personally without drowning it in explanation and qualifications—is one of the prerequisites for marriage counseling. You will be most ready to start mutual marriage counseling when you have seen God deliver you from defensiveness and blame shifting. When you stop trying to even the playing field, you are ready to step onto an even playing field.

There will be a time for each person to consider the old marriage. In what way were we both co-creators of a marriage that left us vulnerable? This is something that can be done together, and blame (for the problems in the marriage) will be shared. But true marriage counseling cannot happen until both spouses are ready to speak of themselves as people who have both been wronged and done wrong. It's hard to improve upon the simple counsel of Jesus to remove the log from our own eyes first (see Matt. 7:5).

Reflect: Am I ready for marriage counseling? Have I put down my weapons and released my impulse to attack and criticize?

Act: Read over Matthew 7:1–5 and consider what the log in your eye is. Ask God to free you to ignore the speck in your spouse's eye until your log is truly dealt with.

QUALITIES AND HABITS FOR THE LONG HAUL

Simply surviving an affair isn't the end goal. You want to be a new person who is characterized by a new way of living. Several qualities and habits emerge as you walk in the way of Jesus. You become more patient. You reengage with people in unassuming, non-entitled ways. You earn trust. You have learned to face what is really in the mirror and to take restorative action. You aren't fragile, begging for affirmation and compliments, but you are well guarded from despair by knowing who you are and whose you are. You know that Jesus's promise is strong and that He is not done with you. He will finish what He has started in you (see Phil. 1:6).

DAY 21

Patience

Who among you fears the LORD and obeys the voice of his servant? Let him who walks in darkness and has no light trust in the name of the LORD and rely on his God. (Isa. 50:10)

I KNOW A man who experienced his greatest sexual temptations while serving overnight work shifts. His only task was to stay awake and be on call. You can imagine how much he anticipated seeing light first come through the window. In ancient times, people felt this sense of painful waiting and eager anticipation during night watches. David says that he waits on God "more than watchmen wait for the morning" (Ps. 130:6 NIV). His relationship with God requires patience (as do all relationships), as he waits and longs for something good.

Being patient through hard feelings is one of the hardest things for someone to do. In fact, your not being able to sit through hard emotions was a contributing factor in the affair itself. *A sexual failure is always first a failure of patience.* Impatience will also be one of your greatest obstacles as you seek to reconcile with your spouse. You will likely think you have been very patient at precisely the moment when you need to continue being patient. At that point you will have already been more patient than you've ever been before. So it is both good news (you're pushing your limit!) and bad news (you still have to hang in there!).

Your patience will be need to be evident both in the process of healing (as you comply for the duration of your church's recommended care plan, with the recommended counseling, and with your spouse's requests), and also toward your spouse, who may not see the evidence that you are changing (especially at times when you feel that you have made gains).

Patience will also be required during conversations with your spouse. Part of your spouse's healing process will be to learn not to try to punish you, but it will not be *your* role to lead your spouse through that process. Likely you will feel weighed down and beaten up, and it will be hard for you to endure. Seek to ask questions—for example, "Has it been a really hard day?" or "Have I done something more that's really hurting right now?" Statements of feeling can sometimes be okay, such as "I hate that I've hurt you this bad," or "I'm sure I don't know what I've put you through, and I am genuinely willing to listen so that I can try to feel this with you."

Watch out for the opposite of patience: *anger*. Anger is a response to a sense of injustice, dishonor, or lack of control. You will feel dishonored. You will likely also feel that you're being treated unfairly at some point in the process of reconciliation. You will likely feel distress when you do not have control over the reconciliation process. This is a perfect recipe for anger. Yet gentleness and patience will show that you are changing.

As much as you eagerly anticipate a new day, God is calling you to endure faithfully. And He is eager to meet with you. The best thing that you are impatient for doesn't compare to the reward for those who wait upon the Lord: renewed strength, transcendence, eagles' wings (see Isa. 40:31). Waiting on Him does not bring you to shame (Ps. 25:3). For Him we "wait all the day long" (Ps. 25:5).

Reflect: Where else in your life do you see impatience? Progress in any of these areas will make for progress in your struggle against sexual sin and in the restoration work for your marriage.

Act: Ask the Lord for a generous, patient heart toward your spouse and toward the process of healing.

DAY 22

Becoming Trustworthy

Since we have been justified by faith, we have peace with God through our Lord Jesus Christ. . . . We rejoice in our sufferings, knowing that suffering produces endurance, and endurance produces character, and character produces hope, and hope does not put us to shame. (Rom. 5:1, 3–5)

SINCE THERE IS no shortcut to character, the way to demonstrate a new, faithful way of life is over time. This is nearly always harder than we imagine. Endurance comes through suffering (see Rom. 5:3) and leads to character—a proven trustworthiness. But it starts with knowing where our ultimate vindication and "rightness" come from. If we can know the wonder of our justification and peace with God, we will be less consumed with the drive to justify ourselves before others.

You will feel your patience tested when you are not trusted and not viewed as someone with reliable character. You will want to feel right in the eyes of others. To be questioned and accused feels like an insult. *Haven't I done hard things? Aren't I doing anything right? Are you saying that nothing has changed? Don't you believe me?*[1]

Let me encourage you not to interpret your spouse's hesitation as signifying that nothing you have done has made a difference. Don't rush to an all-or-nothing vindication of your efforts. You have done a lot, yes—but there is still much to do. You may find yourself giving blanket assurances, promises, and pledges. These are not always wrong, but they can't form the majority of your approach. Ask your spouse to talk about *how* the relationship does not feel safe rather than assuring him or her that it *is* safe. You want your words to have a welcoming rather than a dismissing tone. Assurances often make your spouse feel as if the offense is just being swept under the rug. Or the assurance can make the sting of the offense worse, because it invites the immediate question "If you lied to me about the affair, how can I ever know you aren't lying to me now?"

All my advice about confession so far requires a lot of exposure and vulnerability, and that requires *trust*. Your survival in the healing process will require that you let others in, not just your spouse. The Bible teaches both independence (see Gal. 6:5) and interdependence (see Eph. 4:15–16). What can you say or do that will continue to invite others into your life?

This openness is definitely uncomfortable. Dig deep into the confidence that you gain from knowing that God stands by you—if He is at peace with you, conflict or disapproval will be much less scary. To borrow from Ed Welch's saying, when God is big to us, people's criticisms are small.[2]

Becoming a trustworthy spouse, and growing in trusting others, first requires trust in the Lord and in His ability to lead you from suffering to endurance, from endurance to character, and from character to hope. So don't lean on your own understanding (see Prov. 3:5–6). Even now He pours His love into your heart (see Rom. 5:5). He wants what is best for you. He is worthy of all our trust.

Reflect: Do you find that your assurances and promises to your spouse are hurtful or helpful?

Reflect: Are there things you've been holding back from your support team (see day 9)?

Act: Do you find yourself exasperated when your spouse expresses a lack of trust in you and in your word? Invite God to grow character in you as you continue to endure this distress.

DAY 23

Unassuming Reengagement

*Every good gift and every perfect gift is from above, coming
down from the Father of lights, with whom there is no
variation or shadow due to change. (James 1:17)*

WHEN YOU HAVE begun to walk in the light and have made
progress, you naturally want others to rejoice with you. It can
become tempting to start to feel a sense that your spouse is being
unfair in holding back and keeping distance, or in not opening
the door to reconciliation. In this painful place of uncertainty and
change, James invites us to see the steady and unchanging God,
along with His good gifts—the kindnesses from Him that are as
unearned and undeserved as our salvation.

It will be important for you to believe that closeness with
your spouse is a privilege to be offered rather than a right to be
demanded.[1] At times, under the surface, you will likely feel that
it is only fair to be close to him or her, that you've earned it, and
that in fact you deserve it. But even if it were true, it would have
as much romantic effect on the relationship as a courtroom conversation between lawyers. You have to be in a mindset that you
would be lucky to have your spouse back.

If you're not sure how to muster that feeling, then you're close
to understanding how hopeless you are to change course without
miraculous help from the Spirit of God.

This is another way of saying that you must understand grace.
God is good, kind, generous beyond belief. But He will not exist
in a relationship of demand with His creation. We cannot pull a
lever and call down His blessings by our behavior. Closeness in
relationship is a freely offered gift, not something to be demanded
or wrestled from someone. The one person in the whole world

who could demand or force closeness does not, but rather invites and wins us through His love.[2]

If your spouse comes close to you again, it will be a good gift from God. If your mindset becomes one in which you are excited to have your spouse back again and are not looking to settle scores, this will be a good gift from God. Pray for these gifts, and receive them as from Him.

Reflect: Can you find feelings of entitlement persisting in yourself? Do you feel that you've earned and deserve a close relationship?

Act: Ask a friend, counselor, or pastor whether he or she gets the impression from you that you're operating out of a sense of what you feel owed or what you feel are your rights. This is vital feedback to receive. Expect to hear ways that you are unintentionally speaking out of a sense of entitlement.

DAY 24

Resting in God's Vindication

Hear a just cause, O LORD; attend to my cry! Give ear to
my prayer from lips free of deceit! From your presence let my
vindication come! Let your eyes behold the right! (Ps. 17:1–2)

IT WILL CONTINUE to be very tempting for you to plead your
cause—to represent yourself in court, so to say. But seeing your
vindication as coming from God will help you not to try to control your spouse and will dignify and honor your spouse as one
who is capable of choosing and sifting counsel.

You may feel highly threatened when your spouse gets advice
or reads books. You want him or her to see things a certain way—
likely you have specific views on how reconciliation should happen, why you should now be trusted, why your spouse should
now listen and believe you. You want to be vindicated in your
spouse's eyes.

Yet we must learn to pray this way: *Lord, if I am to be in the right*
and my words are to be right, let it be your doing alone. In Psalm 17,
vindication comes from the Lord. It's not your words, thoughts,
and plans that you can trust to defend yourself. Entrust yourself,
your spouse, and your marriage to the Lord—the Judge whose
verdict and vindication carry ultimate weight.

If your spouse has closed the door on the possibility of reconciliation, these kinds of reflections and prayers are still an important step. You will likely feel the temptation to suggest that it was
someone's bad advice that ruined things for you, rather than your
spouse's decision. Here's why this is a problem: adultery happens
due to a pervasive self-centeredness combined with a lack of
concern and respect for your spouse. Often this is all combined
with a deep resentment toward your spouse. To suggest that your

spouse was led astray or deceived by bad advice paints a negative picture of your spouse. It paints a picture of a naive, easily fooled person who would do better if only he or she would listen to you. This is the attitude you convey when you attack the help that your spouse has received. This is also the attitude conveyed by deception and infidelity itself. It's a continuation of the same mindset that led to the original problem.

Reflect: In what ways are you tempted to vindicate yourself?

Act: Have you found yourself ruminating negatively about your spouse? Invite God to direct your thoughts to more loving and productive meditations.

DAY 25

Moving On

"Yet even now," declares the Lord, *"return to me with all your heart, with fasting, with weeping, and with mourning; and rend your hearts and not your garments." Return to the* Lord *your God, for he is gracious and merciful, slow to anger, and abounding in steadfast love. (Joel 2:12–13)*

In today's passage, Joel calls for deep repentance (v. 12), not for a religious performance that is over quickly and forgotten. What God desires is a tearing of your heart, not a hollow religious act of tearing your garment (v. 13). Your heart is capable of duplicity—you may do the right things on the outside but have a heart that is far from God. This is a season to return to the Lord with tender emotions and to grieve sin. That posture is incompatible with focusing on how someone else needs to move on from being upset with you.

Repentance changes your posture toward your spouse. Your spouse will certainly need help moving toward forgiveness, but it will not be your task to lead this process. Your responsibility will be similar to what you are asking of your spouse for yourself: patience and grace. Forgiveness will not be a one-time thing; it will be a process of entrusting to God your many different feelings of anger, rejection, shame, and much more.

Many people during this season feel or say something like this: *There is no sense in dwelling on the past.* You may feel this many times. But it will continue to be important for you to remain submitted to the process rather than to direct the process (see day 11). It will feel like dwelling on the past when it is really taking a hard look at where you have been *so that you don't stay there.* Yes, you do move on. The goal is redemptive—but you have to know what is being redeemed.

Other statements that indicate an attempt to move on too quickly are ones such as "I'm more interested in where we're headed than in where we've been" or "You said you forgave me, so why won't you let it go?" These kinds of statements arise from two feelings: (1) a sincere longing to live the restored life and (2) a false sense that you are aware of the seriousness of the offense.

To criticize another person's desire to talk about the past is typically a self-protective move. It is unpleasant to talk about pain we have caused. You may also believe that preventing your spouse from talking about past pains will protect him or her from bitterness. Sadly, this is rarely the effect. If you find yourself critical of your spouse for wanting to talk about the past, make more effort to understand the impact of your infidelity on him or her. Genuine repentance demonstrates humility by being willing to have hard conversations about the past.

When you find yourself feeling this, hurry to the Lord. He is ready and willing to do a work in you emotionally so that your heart is "rent" and is ready to be gentle with your spouse's process of healing. This is the fastest, surest way to move on.

Reflect: Are you willing to welcome conversation about the past in this season, however painful it is?

Act: The warning from Joel comes in the face of God's judgment of locusts in Joel 1. Joel 2:12 starts with "Even now"— a warning to Judah to turn from sin and return to the Lord. Even now, I invite you, turn to Him and repent. Come back to Him. He is eager to bless us when we turn: "I am sending you grain, new wine and olive oil, enough to satisfy you fully; never again will I make you an object of scorn" (Joel 2:19 NIV).

DAY 26

Facing the Mirror

The one who looks into the perfect law, the law of liberty,
and perseveres, being no hearer who forgets but a doer who
acts, he will be blessed in his doing. (James 1:25)

IN THE MOVIE *Premonition*, a little girl runs into a glass door so hard that she breaks it and cuts her face severely. Her mother doesn't want her daughter to be upset by how bad her face looks, so she covers all the mirrors in the home while it heals.

We all have scratches and cuts and stitches that we would rather not look at. We have cut ourselves up and disfigured ourselves by living in unloving ways. Ugly actions make us morally ugly. And so, naturally, it's a little more bearable for us to simply cover up the mirrors around us. One of the best ways to do this is to cover over anything that shows us ourselves as we really are. Often that includes people who tell us the hard truth about ourselves.

One writer says that affairs offer us the kind of mirror that distorts reality and makes us look really good. "We like how we see ourselves reflected in the other person's eyes. By contrast, in our long-term relationships, our reflection is like a 5x makeup mirror in which our flaws are magnified. In a new romance, our reflection is like the rosy glow of an illuminated vanity mirror."[1]

We all know this. In our marriages we are regularly faced with our imperfections. But in a new relationship, you get to see yourself without those flaws. You can look into the vanity mirror and see that you aren't the terrible person that you feel like in your marriage. You're the kind of person who someone would fall in love with. Why should you not have the happiness that other people have? . . . You see how it works.

The reason you are reading a devotional is that you believe there is a mirror that is far better than what a new romance or old marriage shows you. It's the "perfect law of liberty." And it does show you the ugly truth. It shows you as you really are. But it doesn't leave you there. If you act on what you hear (becoming a "doer of the Word"), if you refuse to look away from the true mirror but instead let it show you what needs to change, you will find great blessing. This blessedness actually changes what you see in the mirror, over time.

If the Lord really is remaking each one of us after the image of His Son, then someday we will share in His glory. We will one day see something full of glory in the mirror. Yet "the bride eyes not her garment, but her dear bridegroom's face; I will not gaze at glory, but on my King of grace."[2]

One of the reasons Paul urges us to run away from sexual sin is that it doesn't fit with who God is making us into. You get rid of sin as a result of "seeing that you have put off the old self with its practices and have put on the new self, which is being renewed in knowledge after the image of its creator" (Col. 3:9–10).

> **Reflect:** Did the relationship outside your marriage allow you to see yourself in a way that you liked? What were you longing for? Who were you longing to be?
>
> **Act:** (1) Ask God to bring you to His glory through Jesus, and repent of seeking a glory and identity apart from Him. (2) What flaws in yourself do the mirrors of God's Word and your marriage regularly show you? Run to Jesus in your imperfection and flaws!

DAY 27

Shedding Shame and Finding Mercy

"O my God, I am ashamed and blush to lift my face to you.... After all that has come upon us for our evil deeds ... seeing that you, our God, have punished us less than our iniquities deserved.... We are before you in our guilt, for none can stand before you because of this." (Ezra 9:6, 13, 15)

THE JUSTICE OF God requires punishment for sins (see Ezra 9:15). It would be fair for His righteous anger to consume us (see v. 14). Yet in Ezra we find that God's consequences are less than what we deserve (see v. 13). God knows all our sin, but He treats us better than we deserve.

This mindset is a powerful antidote to the frustration that you may be feeling if people in your life aren't welcoming you with open arms. You will likely be tempted to launch a counterattack: *Okay, I'm no saint, but people around me are so hypocritical.*

This is an important time to reflect on the nature of your forgiveness and reconciliation process with your spouse. There is a difference between how God forgives and how your spouse may forgive. God forgives immediately. He doesn't wait to see whether you've changed before embracing you. He won't leave you unchanged, but He does welcome you home while you're a long way from perfect.

God's experience of your sin was very different from your spouse's. God saw the small steps you were taking—browsing through Facebook profiles, having small conversations at work, feeling that it was only very minimally inappropriate to go to coffee. God also saw your opportunities to turn back. He provided many ways of escape. He saw you crossing each boundary, and He grieved because He loves you. And He didn't stay far away, even after you missed the ways of escape. He invited you back.

Your spouse had a very different experience. The marriage, your family, dinner, family pictures, dates, Christmas morning—all these things came together to create a picture of a status quo. Things weren't perfect, but they were predictable. The same conflicts. The same kinds of distance, efforts to connect, good and bad times.

It's common for the offended spouse to feel that the deception was worse than whatever happened sexually or emotionally outside the marriage. Deception invites a betrayed spouse to rethink everything. And this is hugely disorienting. My experience is that most Christian spouses are open to starting the process of reconciliation. But it always requires knowing what is up and what is down, what is true and what is not. After a long season of deception, this is highly challenging.

Honest admission is best paired with the tone that we see in Ezra. It makes you blush. You stop talking about the bitterness of others, because you are so aware that you have been in the wrong. You start to see the devastation that sin causes, and you start to see the distance in your relationships as part of this devastation. But being able to face our guilt before the Lord (see v. 15) creates a profound and quieting humility.

> **Reflect:** Your spouse's disorientation requires your patience. Human forgiveness is a process. Consider God's generosity and mercy toward you in this season, and invite Him to lead you toward generosity and mercy for those who struggle to forgive you.
>
> **Act:** Consider whether you need to offer a few comments to your spouse or family in order to release them from feeling any pressure to move toward forgiveness or closeness before they feel ready. Admit that you do not understand their experience, but begin trying to understand it.

DAY 28

Ongoing Openness

God is light, and in him is no darkness at all. If we say we have fellowship with him while we walk in darkness, we lie and do not practice the truth. But if we walk in the light, as he is in the light, we have fellowship with one another, and the blood of Jesus his Son cleanses us from all sin. (1 John 1:5–7)

THERE IS NO darkness or evil in God (see 1 John 1:5). He is pure light and moral perfection. In His light we find forgiveness and fellowship—closeness with Him and with others. It is incompatible for us to say that we have stepped into His light while living in darkness and deception (see v. 6). If we hide, or try to live in both the darkness and the light, we live a lie. But to walk in the light is to walk a path toward integrity, connection, and cleansing (see v. 7; cf. Prov. 28:13). So choose light, not darkness! Easy choice, right?

Light is exposing and uncomfortable. I hate turning on the light first thing in the morning. But it is much safer, and I save myself a lot of stumbling around. Light is also life-giving. A lot of plants don't grow well in the shade. The Christian life is like that—growth happens best in full sun. Try to remember that the discomfort of honesty is life-giving, and even restorative to relationships. It ends with us having fellowship with each other and with God, who cleanses all sin (see Ps. 51:7–10).

Affairs are impossible without some kind of hiding. Hiding necessarily created protective distance between you and the person closest to you: your spouse. You've learned over time to keep certain walls up, to be seen as strong. But weakness and vulnerability are your two best friends right now. They are intimidating, and you will hate having them around—but they are central pieces of the healing process. It is painful to be open. It is risky, and it makes us feel vulnerable and exposed.

Here is the rationale for painful openness: it is a way for our love to look more like God's love. God in Christ was vulnerable, leaving the safety of heaven and coming into our world at cost to Himself. His sacrifice was necessary in order to create closeness of relationship with us. So it is with us. We sacrifice our sense of safe distance in order to be close to someone else.

If you have not done good things in secrecy, your spouse will be uncomfortable with secrecy for a long time—even if you are not doing anything wrong in private. You are welcome to have opinions about what your spouse should and should not have access to technology-wise, but unless you grant your spouse access to your phone, email, social media, and so on, then you can expect him or her to find it difficult to trust you. This will be an area in which you'll face a trade off: *Would I like my spouse to be close to me, love me, and trust me? Or would I like to have safe distance and privacy?* I see too many people fighting for privacy in marriage when a dose of exposure and openness would actually create the preconditions for closeness and healing.

Reflect: What patterns of hiding and concealing remain in your behavior? What small things do you find yourself hesitant to mention to accountability partners?

Act: Ask your pastor, counselor, or friend for feedback on your level of transparency. Talk with God about ways that you find yourself drawn to hide.

DAY 29

A New Name and Identity

*Or do you not know that the unrighteous will not inherit the
kingdom of God? Do not be deceived: neither the sexually
immoral, nor idolaters, nor adulterers . . . will inherit the kingdom
of God. And such were some of you. But you were washed, you
were sanctified, you were justified in the name of the Lord Jesus
Christ and by the Spirit of our God. (1 Cor. 6:9–11)*

WHOLE-IDENTITY PHRASES AND name-calling can be very
painful. No one likes labels. When the Bible uses whole-identity
phrases such as drunkard, swindler, and adulterer, they are, for
believers, in the past tense. You *were* this, but that's not the final
word. God's grace creates *new* identity markers, new names. You
were once an adulterer: "such were some of you." But then you
were changed through the work of the Spirit that brought you to
faith in Christ—*from* adulterer *to* washed, sanctified, and justified.

Paul was willing to call himself the lowest of sinners: "Christ
Jesus came into the world to save sinners—of whom I am the
worst" (1 Tim. 1:15 NIV). He was even willing to detail his sins.
But no one would ever get the impression that he was either stuck
in despair or unwilling to let someone call him a murderer. He
was first and foremost "Paul in Christ" or "Paul the Christian."
He was secure in this new and greater identity. Other people's
name-calling could not crush him.

I am arguing for you to have two attitudes, to be expressed in
different areas.

1. *To keep in your heart:* There was a time when it would have
   been true to say "I am an adulterer." But, by the grace of God,
   that is no longer true. This attitude guards against becoming "overwhelmed by excessive sorrow" (2 Cor. 2:7).

2. *To express to others:* "You are justified in calling me all kinds of things, and I will not argue with you. I am the chief of sinners. God have mercy on me." This attitude guards against minimizing your offense to others.

It can be very hard to grapple with the reality of having failed in this area. Every time I counsel people who are guilty of a sexual offense, they feel that they are being treated unfairly by others (or by the law) and being seen as special kinds of sinners—as a unique kind of bad. One of the deepest, most abiding struggles you will likely face is the shame and embarrassment of people knowing about your failings. Infidelity often causes big, visible problems. But let me encourage you not to let shame set the course for your relationships. Push past the embarrassment and talk with people out of a well-placed, humble confidence. This freedom from shame comes with embracing your new identity as the prized possession of our Father—one who has been bought "with the precious blood of Christ" (1 Peter 1:19).

Reflect: Where do you see shame pulling you away from people? From God?

Act: Consider getting familiar with "identity statements" that will encourage you, such as this one from Martin Luther: "[Satan would say,] 'Martin, you are a liar, greedy, lecherous, a blasphemer, a hypocrite. You cannot stand before God.' To which Luther would respond: 'Well, yes, I am. And, indeed, Satan, you do not know the half of it. . . . But you know what? My Saviour has died for all my sins. . . . His blood is sufficient; and on the Day of Judgment I shall be exonerated because he has taken all my sins on himself and clothed me in his own perfect righteousness.'"[1]

80

DAY 30

Avoiding the Downward Spiral

So you should rather turn to forgive and comfort him,
or he may be overwhelmed by excessive sorrow. So I beg
you to reaffirm your love for him. (2 Cor. 2:7–8)

SEXUAL SIN HAS the power to numb us to reality. With some practice, it's possible for us to live and perform at a reasonably high level while at the same time burying a dark secret. Sexual sin is both the dark secret and a shield to keep others from seeing the dark secret accurately.

When people first turn back to the Lord and come into the light, they often feel a strong sense of relief. *Wow—how wonderful it is to be free of this burden, to no longer hide!* There's often a drop-off in temptation in the early months. In the early stages of recovery, old sin can look ugly and undesirable. Maybe you are experiencing this. You haven't started to miss it yet. It's a honeymoon period to be thankful for.

Once you stop contacting an old love interest or viewing pornography, eventually you will start to feel some rough emotions. If you continue to keep fantasies active in your mind, they might delay coming back to reality in your emotions. But if you don't numb yourself, eventually feelings will come—and not very nicely. Typically you will feel annoyance, irritation, frustration, angst, fear, sadness, despair. You don't have the escape that used to get you through life. And it doesn't feel very good. It gets discouraging to feel so weak.

Those who are walking the faithful path after sexual sin are in danger of crippling discouragement. In 2 Corinthians 2, Paul follows up on 1 Corinthians 5, where he called the Corinthians to practice church discipline on a man who was living in sexual sin. But now that the man has repented, there is a danger that he will be "overwhelmed by excessive sorrow." The harshness of others will weigh him down. He needs the church to offer forgiveness, comfort, and love. Otherwise he will be vulnerable to discouragement and, even worse, despair.

When you see your situation more clearly, you realize the pain you have caused. You realize the consequences that are coming, and you experience the ones that have already started. And you feel emotions that you didn't always feel along the way, during the affair. The spark and excitement of the relationship that made you feel so alive is gone. You're left with a burned-down house, and you know it was your fire that got out of control. This new awareness can lead to a downward spiral of despair.

Some heavy emotions will be normal in this season. Aim for an extremely difficult middle way. *(1) Avoid turning conversations of other people's pain into conversations about your own pain.* This is hard not to do. When you hear family members talk about the impact of the infidelity, do everything you can to be with them in their pain and to validate it. You can certainly share what you feel about it, but do not bring the focus of the conversation onto your pain. *(2) Avoid tactics of escaping from heavy feelings.* This can mean good things carried to excess (media, food, distraction) or things that are bad in themselves (argumentativeness, defensiveness, forced positivity). Sit with godly sorrow, because it leads to change (see 2 Cor. 7:10). Remember that "the LORD is near to the brokenhearted and saves the crushed in spirit" (Ps. 34:18).

Reflect: Are you tempted either to turn conversations into a dialogue about your own pain or to avoid your heavy feelings?

Act: Ask those who are close to you if it's been difficult for them to talk honestly with you about their pain.

DAY 31

Pure and Joyful

But you, beloved . . . keep yourselves in the love of God, waiting for the mercy of our Lord Jesus Christ that leads to eternal life. . . . Now to him who is able to keep you from stumbling and to present you blameless before the presence of his glory with great joy, to the only God, our Savior, through Jesus Christ our Lord, be glory, majesty, dominion, and authority, before all time and now and forever. Amen. (Jude 20–21, 24–25)

IN THE STORIES of Israel's wilderness wanderings, the people of God needed something to eat every day. So God sent them manna every day. There was enough for every person, every day. But no one could save more for the next day or week. They were dependent upon Him for every meal. This is how God sustains His people: He provides His grace daily. The dependence required of us the first time we bow our knees is the same dependence required of every successive time we bow. "'Tis grace has brought me safe thus far, and grace will lead me home."[1] Receiving this grace from Him daily is the way to build ourselves up in our most holy faith—we pray in the Holy Spirit, stay close to the love of the Father, and patiently wait and depend on the mercy of Christ. This is the way of life (see Jude 20–21).

Pastors often recite these verses as the benediction at the end of a worship service. These are hopeful words—words to give us hope and excitement as we walk out the door and go forth to serve the world, as those called by the name of Christ. It's a hope that is meant to go deep into our bones. And what is the hope? That one day He will present us "blameless before the presence of his glory with great joy" (Jude 25). The presence of His glory is a fearful place—our God is a consuming fire (see Heb. 12:29), and to be full of sin and blame in the face of glory is terrifying.

We already know what it is like to be full of sin in front of other people. We hate it. It feels awful. How much worse to be sinful in front of a holy God? He has to prepare us for that day.

There is an old hymn that says, "He died that we might be forgiv'n, *he died to make us good*."² The Christian's hope is that it will one day be an accurate statement that *you* are a good person. God has adopted you into His family. He has justified you—made you righteous in His sight by crediting your sin to Jesus and His righteousness to you. But one day the work of sanctification will be complete. You will actually *be* holy—a saint; one set apart to God. You will be pure and good and happy. And you will testify, as Paul, that though you worked very hard, it was "not I, but the grace of God that [was] with me" (1 Cor. 15:10).

Reflect: What do you wish people would say about you on your annual review at work? What do you wish your spouse and kids would say about the kind of person you are? What do you wish people would say at your funeral someday? Consider that God is working now to make those things true of you. He won't give up the work that He has started until He is done (see Phil. 1:6).

Act: Add your amen to Jude's benediction: *O Lord, let it be so!* Ask God to continue to sanctify you; to make you one of His saints, both in name and in practice; to bring you to the Holy One's presence as one of His holy ones.

Conclusion

I WISH WE could sit down together, because I'd like to speak to you for a moment and give you some final encouragement. Many next steps and tasks have come up over these brief pages. I will leave you with a few core things. Share your sorrows with God, and talk to Him early and often. Keep a team of people around you who can pray and help you to stay the course. Make full use of the resources available to you: pastors, friends, counselors, books, podcasts, and anything else that edifies you. Make every effort to live in the light. Admit failures along the way, even if you're afraid that admitting them will cost you everything. It's your only chance at keeping anything. Continue as a student of those who are in pain. Don't look away from the impact of your actions, but invite those who are close to you to share about that impact. Think creatively about the impact you have had, so that others don't have to do all the work to explain it and so that you can constructively move toward them. This alone will be healing—though there is much left to do. Beg God for patient endurance. Ask Him to return to you the joy of your salvation and to uphold you with a willing spirit (see Ps. 51:12).

If you have actually taken those steps, and tried to do all the right things, you still might feel much worse. You are feeling more of the weight of it all. You are starting to get it. You now see the massive collateral damage of something that, at the moment, didn't seem to be all that big of a deal.

All these new habits and insights are vital. And all this may make you feel burdened, stressed, and even a little panicked. Maybe at this point you feel the urgency of changing everything quickly. Steps can't be taken fast enough. How do you hold on to passion for change and trust in God's timing? How do you stay motivated to work hard when the results are not guaranteed? How do you embrace humility without falling into despair?

There's no mantra to fix those feelings. But don't numb them. Bring them to the Lord and let them be shaped by His heart. What grieves Him? Let it grieve us. What is His hope for the world? Let it be ours. This is one way that we will feel close to Him in this season. And this closeness will hold us through many long and lonely nights.

His nearness is good for us (see Ps. 73:28). One of the benefits of being close to our Father in heaven is that He brings a deep and abiding sense of peace and rest.[1] And His rest is powerful for defeating our self-reliant urgency, impatience, frustration, and stressed-out despair.

"Let us therefore strive to enter that rest" (Heb. 4:11). And who leads us there? Look to the One who lived and worked and rested perfectly—who could always be interrupted to help one more person while also being on His way to the mountains to rest and be close with His Father. *Our Father.*

Some of the best pictures we have for understanding God are family pictures. What is this closeness and rest that God offers to us? Maybe we can say this: it's sitting in a big cozy chair on a Saturday morning after a long week of work, sipping coffee and chatting with your spouse while your kids pop in and out, goofing off and asking questions and giving hugs. There's a lot that needs to be done, and that's faithful stewardship. But there's no urgency that should get in the way of this. So it is with God, the Lover of our souls and the Father of us, His children. You are eager to put all this behind you. *Amen. May it always be so!* But let no urgency rush you past the sweet and restful moments with your Father in heaven. These He offers to you now. These He gives you when you start the walk home—when He sees you off in the distance and runs to you, hugs you, and throws a party. He is so excited to have you home.

Acknowledgments

THANK YOU TO Ian and the P&R team for allowing me to be part of the 31-Day Devotionals for Life series. Deepak Reju's work in crafting the series created a template that made the proposal and writing process remarkably smooth, and his feedback made this text decidedly more devotional.

I'm grateful to the many people who came to counseling and allowed me into the private and painful spaces of their lives— where God was working powerfully. People found small and creative ways forward, forging connections and gaining insights from all kinds of places. God broke through. In those relationships I learned that my hard work would never change anyone, so the best I could offer was faithful effort toward competent, loving care. *Kyrie eleison.*

The Christian Counseling and Education Foundation provided me the opportunity to present some of this material first at their 2017 national conference, and several people provided helpful feedback as I prepared. Conversations with Todd Stryd, Aaron Sironi, and Darby Strickland at different junctures shaped key aspects of my perspectives on marriage counseling in the contexts that this book addresses. Mike Emlet's mentoring has been both affirming and challenging and has made me (I hope) wiser and more grounded in the good news of Jesus. His encouragements and initiative to create or connect me with opportunities have shaped the direction of my career, and I owe him much.

Dr. Penny Freeman has been an excellent supervisor throughout my counseling licensure process, and her insights throughout years of mentoring are reflected here in some ways I am aware of, and everywhere else in ways I am not aware of. Without Penny I would be much more ignorant and much less bold in counseling. Eamon Wilson and Joel Bassett have been my close companions in everything that I think and write about, and their friendship has "doubled my joys and halved my sorrows."

Every year I learn a little more how abnormal my normal Christian family is, and every year I am more grateful for parents, grandparents, and great-grandparents who love, and loved, for the long haul of quiet faithfulness. They also prayed I would find a godly wife, and God answered this prayer over and above. Kelly is the greatest friend, confidante, co-parent, and spiritual companion I could have asked for. Her questions, clarifications, and constant encouragement to "take them to Christ" make every sermon, lecture, and article of mine more grounded and hopeful. I thank God, too, for two sons who (although the nursery rhyme doesn't see boys as capable of this) add "sugar and spice and everything nice" to my life every day.

Notes

Tips for Reading This Devotional

1. Jonathan Leeman, *Reverberation: How God's Word Brings Light, Freedom, and Action to His People* (Chicago, Moody, 2011), 19.

Introduction

1. If you have been abused in your marriage, or have suffered abuse in childhood, this book is not the first place to start.

   If you have questions about whether your marriage has been affected by abusive dynamics, consider Leslie Vernick's brief self-assessment "Are You In An Emotionally Destructive Relationship?" from *The Emotionally Destructive Relationship: Seeing It, Stopping It, Surviving It* (Eugene, OR: Harvest House, 2007), chap. 1, available online at https://www.leslievernick.com/pdfs/Relationship-test.pdf; as well as her book *The Emotionally Destructive Marriage: How to Find Your Voice and Reclaim Your Hope* (Colorado Springs: WaterBrook, 2013).

   If you have experienced childhood sexual abuse, I would encourage you to consider individual counseling first, as well as to pick up a book such as Diane Langberg's *On the Threshold of Hope: Opening the Door to Healing for Survivors of Sexual Abuse* (Carol Stream, IL: Tyndale House, 1999).

2. Many Christian resources on infidelity are either the testimonials of men (or of couples in which the husband has cheated) or the work of counselors who write primarily from their experience working with men (such as this book). The resources have not caught up with new trends; because, per one study, "Among ever-married adults ages 18 to 29, women are slightly more likely than men to be guilty of infidelity" (Wendy Wang, "Who Cheats More? The Demographics of Infidelity in America," Institute for Family Studies, January 10, 2018, https://ifstudies.org/blog/who-cheats-more-the-demographics-of-cheating-in-america).

   Some secular authors speak with greater focus on patterns

of infidelity that are more commonly seen in women. See, for example, Esther Perel, *The State of Affairs: Rethinking Infidelity* (New York: HarperCollins, 2017) and Michelle Langley, *Women's Infidelity: Living in Limbo; What Women Really Mean When They Say "I'm Not Happy"* (St. Louis: McCarlan, 2005). To locate Christian resources for women, I recommend Harvest USA—see, for example, Ellen Dykas's article series "Emotional Affairs: When Closeness Becomes Destructive" (three articles that you can search for at https://www.harvestusa.org).

3. Esther Perel, "Rethinking Infidelity: A Talk for Anyone Who Has Ever Loved," filmed March 19, 2015, in Vancouver, TED video, 21:31, https://www.ted.com/talks/esther_perel_rethinking _infidelity_a_talk_for_anyone_who_has_ever_loved. Perel also offers her approach to infidelity counseling, and in more depth, in her article "Why Happy People Cheat," *The Atlantic*, October 2017, https://www.theatlantic.com/magazine/archive/2017/10/why -happy-people-cheat/537882/.

Also see Russell Moore's brief but helpful Christian assessment of Perel's approach, "Will a Happy Marriage Prevent an Affair?" The Ethics and Religious Liberty Commission of the Southern Baptish Convention, September 14, 2017, https://www.russell moore.com/2017/09/14/will-happy-marriage-prevent-affair/.

Day 3: Knowing the Healer

1. The hymn continues, "Let not conscience make you linger, nor of fitness fondly dream; all the fitness he requireth is to feel your need of Him" (Joseph Hart, "Come, Ye Sinners, Poor and Needy," 1759).

2. George Herbert's poem "Love (3)" is a beautiful picture of human hesitation being met with Divine invitation. God invites us to His table, and it is not a time to be part of the wait staff. Our call is to sit at His table, and His promise is to make us into worthy guests (see George Herbert, *The Complete English Works* [New York: Alfred A. Kopf, 1995], 184).

Day 5: Sinners, Poor and Needy

1. Joseph Hart, "Come, Ye Sinners, Poor and Needy," 1759.

2. See Meredith Masony, "Life Is Short. Have an Affair," *HuffPost*, July

21, 2015, http://www.huffingtonpost.com/meredith-masony/life
-is-short-have-an-aff_1_b_7833874.html.

3. The Greek word for *temptation* is the same word for *trial* or *test* (*peirasmos*), and it captures the fact that all enticement to sin is both alluring and afflicting. To be tempted as a Christian is to suffer. For more on this point see my seminar "Emotions and Sexual Escape: Reframing the Rescue" (session at the CCEF National Conference, Chattanooga, TN, October 14, 2016), which can be accessed at https://www.ccef.org/shop/product/emotions-sexual-escape -reframing-rescue. For a larger treatment of the afflicting and alluring elements of temptation, see David Powlison, *Making All Things New: Restoring Joy to the Sexually Broken* (Wheaton, IL: Crossway, 2017).

Day 6: Satan's Plans

1. "A Collect for Peace," from Daily Evening Prayer: Rite Two, in the 1979 US version of the *Book of Common Prayer*, available online at http://justus.anglican.org/resources/bcp/ep2.pdf, p. 123.

Day 9: Friends for the Journey

1. I explore this and other transitions in more detail in my seminar "The Long Way Home: Counseling after Infidelity" (session at the CCEF National Conference, Frisco, TX, October 13, 2017), which can be accessed at https://www.ccef.org/shop/product /long-way-home-counseling-infidelity.

Day 11: Trust the Process

1. "Remember that central to the Lord's complaint against the shepherds of Israel was their failure to pursue the sheep who had wandered away" (Timothy Z. Witmer, *The Shepherd Leader: Achieving Effective Shepherding in Your Church* [Phillipsburg, NJ: P&R Publishing, 2010], 173).

2. Robert D. Jones says, "Your pastor or counselor can help you draft this, but the plan must come from you" (*Restoring Your Broken Marriage: Healing after Adultery* [Greensboro, NC: New Growth, 2009], 17).

Day 12: Learning How to Apologize

1. "Daily Morning Prayer," The Anglican Church in North America, last updated January 9, 2018, https://s3.amazonaws.com/acna/00 Morning%20Prayer%2C%201.9.18.pdf. This prayer, and the larger liturgy, is a modernized version based on the 1662 *Book of Common Prayer*.

Day 13: Intent vs. Impact

1. Arterburn and Martinkus give good examples of the destructive mindset that seeks "to placate [your spouse] so you can wiggle off the hook of your transgressions." They suggest naming key aspects of your affair and the impact that each one had—e.g., a hard day that you took out on your family, money that you spent on your paramour, or a workplace where an affair took place, as well as the effects or painful memories associated with each (see Stephen Arterburn and Jason B. Martinkus, *Worthy of Her Trust: What You Need to Do to Rebuild Sexual Integrity and Win Her Back* [Colorado Springs: WaterBrook, 2014], 149).

Day 14: Not Pulling the Rug Out from under Your Spouse

1. See Shirley P. Glass with Jean Coppock Staeheli, *Not "Just Friends": Rebuilding Trust and Recovering Your Sanity After Infidelity* (New York: Free Press, 2004), 86–87. "Injured partners need to know that the affair will be stopped. They also need to know that all of their questions will be answered" (p. 86). Glass does not write from a Christian perspective, but you'll notice that I quote her several times below, because she describes key dynamics of infidelity and its aftermath in marriage. She covers the topic comprehensively for both women and men.

Day 16: Confessing Well

1. See his Ninety-five Theses, thesis 1, quoted in Henry Wace and C. A. Buchheim, eds., *First Principles of the Reformation, or The Ninety-five Theses and the Three Primary Works of Dr. Martin Luther* (London, 1883), 6.

2. This comment assumes that your children already know. For a

concise overview of what to tell (and not tell) children at different ages about infidelity, see Shirley P. Glass with Jean Coppock Staeheli, Not "Just Friends": Rebuilding Trust and Recovering Your Sanity After Infidelity (New York: Free Press, 2004), 329–30. A key point is not to prohibit your children from talking about it with anyone else after you disclose it to them.

3. See Arterburn and Martinkus's helpful list of examples (along with positive alternatives) in Worthy of Her Trust: What You Need to Do to Rebuild Sexual Integrity and Win Her Back (Colorado Springs: WaterBrook, 2014), 121–22.

4. Westminster Confession of Faith, 15.5.

Day 17: God's Narrative

1. Shirley P. Glass with Jean Coppock Staeheli, Not "Just Friends": Rebuilding Trust and Recovering Your Sanity After Infidelity (New York: Free Press, 2004), 61.

Day 22: Becoming Trustworthy

1. Arterburn and Martinkus compare this mindset to a child expecting a treat for doing what he was supposed to do. This is the kind of tough-love message that is important to hear, if you have ears to hear. The affirmation you are craving for taking restorative action may not come in the way or on the timetable you would like. Having others give you the benefit of the doubt, at this stage, is something to be earned over time, not expected or demanded (see Stephen Arterburn and Jason B. Martinkus, Worthy of Her Trust: What You Need to Do to Rebuild Sexual Integrity and Win Her Back [Colorado Springs: WaterBrook, 2014], 53–54, as well as the section "Do Not Demand that She See Progress" on pages 132–34).

2. See Edward T. Welch, When People Are Big and God Is Small: Overcoming Peer Pressure, Codependency, and the Fear of Man (Phillipsburg, NJ: P&R Publishing, 1997).

Day 23: Unassuming Reengagement

1. "Being in close fellowship with someone is not a right, even if both people are Christians. It is a sacred privilege. The apostle Paul

advises us to distance ourselves from people who are continually destructive, especially if their behaviors or attitudes are sinful and unacceptable, both to us and to God (1 Corinthians 5:9–11; 2 Thessalonians 3:6, 14–15)" (Leslie Vernick, "Unconditional Love, Conditional Relationship," American Association of Christian Counselors, January 16, 2014. https://www.aacc.net/2014/01 /16/unconditional-love-conditional-relationship/).

2. Even in the Westminster Confession of Faith, a Calvinistic statement of faith, God is described as wooing people to Himself rather than doing violence to the will of His creation (Westminster Confession of Faith, 3.1).

Day 26: Facing the Mirror

1. Shirley P. Glass with Jean Coppock Staeheli, *Not "Just Friends": Rebuilding Trust and Recovering Your Sanity After Infidelity* (New York: Free Press, 2004), 45. Also consider Ray Carroll's comments in reference to the allure of affairs over social media: "We have to remember that social media is not a reflection of people as they are, typically. It is a reflection of how we want others to see us" ("Is Facebook Ruining Your Marriage?" Fallen Pastor Ministries, August 2, 2017, https://fallenpastor.com/is-facebook-ruining -your-marriage/).

2. Anne R. Cousin, "The Sands of Time Are Sinking," 1857.

Day 29: A New Name and Identity

1. Quoted in Carl Trueman, "Thank God for Bandit Country," *reformation21* (blog), Alliance of Confessing Evangelicals, June 2009. http://www.reformation21.org/thank-god-for-bandit-country. php.

Day 31: Pure and Joyful

1. John Newton, "Amazing Grace," 1779.

2. Cecil Frances Alexander, "There Is a Green Hill Far Away," 1848 (emphasis added).

Conclusion

1. George Herbert's poem "The Pulley" suggests that God intended for our hearts to be restless apart from Him, and that this restlessness would pull our hearts up to Him to find rest in closeness to Him (see George Herbert, *The Complete English Works* [New York: Alfred A. Kopf, 1995], 156). It illustrates Augustine's famous prayer "You have made us for Yourself, and our hearts are restless until they find their rest in You."

Suggested Resources
for Restoration

I HAVE REFERENCED several resources in the endnotes, but here are a few more that I have not quoted from but that you may find helpful.

Hambrick, Brad. "Seminar—False Love: Overcoming Sexual Sin from Pornography to Adultery." January 24, 2012. http://www.brad hambrick.com/falselove/ [This 9-part video lecture series also has a companion series for the spouse not involved in infidelity, available at "Seminar—True Betrayal: Overcoming the Betrayal of Your Spouse's Sexual Sin," February 7, 2012, http://bradhambrick. com/truebetrayal/]

Shriver, Gary, and Mona Shriver. *Unfaithful: Hope and Healing After Infidelity*. 2nd ed. Colorado Springs: David C. Cook, 2009. [This book is a thorough testimonial that captures well the tragic experience of both spouses when one has been unfaithful. Their story ends well, so a couple who are seeking reconciliation may find it hope-giving. Showing the impact of adultery on the betrayed spouse in first-person narrative is one of the book's greatest strengths.]

Smith, Winston. *Help! My Spouse Committed Adultery: First Steps for Dealing with Betrayal*. Greensboro, NC: New Growth, 2008. [This booklet is good for a couple to read early in the process in order to get oriented to some of the challenges of marital restoration. Smith's book *Marriage Matters: Extraordinary Change Through Ordinary Moments* (Greensboro, NC: New Growth, 2010) is also excellent for later in the process when a couple is addressing longer-term marital issues.]

BIBLICAL
COUNSELING
COALITION

The Biblical Counseling Coalition (BCC) is passionate about enhancing and advancing biblical counseling globally. We accomplish this through broadcasting, connecting, and collaborating.

Broadcasting promotes gospel-centered biblical counseling ministries and resources to bring hope and healing to hurting people around the world. We promote biblical counseling in a number of ways: through our *15:14* podcast, website (biblicalcounselingcoalition.org), partner ministry, conference attendance, and personal relationships.

Connecting biblical counselors and biblical counseling ministries is a central component of the BCC. The BCC was founded by leaders in the biblical counseling movement who saw the need for and the power behind building a strong global network of biblical counselors. We introduce individuals and ministries to one another to establish gospel-centered relationships.

Collaboration is the natural outgrowth of our connecting efforts. We truly believe that biblical counselors and ministries can accomplish more by working together. The BCC Confessional Statement, which is a clear and comprehensive definition of biblical counseling, was created through the cooperative effort of over thirty leading biblical counselors. The BCC has also published a three-part series of multi-contributor works that bring theological wisdom and practical expertise to pastors, church leaders, counseling practitioners, and students. Each year we are able to facilitate the production of numerous resources, including books, articles, videos, audio resources, and a host of other helps for biblical counselors. Working together allows us to provide robust resources and develop best practices in biblical counseling so that we can hone the ministry of soul care in the church.

To learn more about the BCC, visit biblicalcounselingcoalition.org.

More Marriage Resources
from P&R Publishing

For better . . . or for worse?

Whichever term describes your marriage, there are ways to make it
(even) better. That's because God has designed marriage to be a relationship of deep unity and strength. Despite the challenges that couples
face today, marital harmony need not be considered an impossible ideal.

Wayne A. Mack recognizes the challenges before us and shows us how
to meet those challenges with growing success. In this book, he has
gathered a wealth of biblical insight and practical information on marital
roles, communication, finances, sex, child-rearing, and family worship.
Both as a counseling aid and as a guide for husbands and wives to study
together, this book offers true hope and help where couples need it most.